AWARD OF MERIT

PRESENTED TO

Richard New

BY THE

WATERLOO COUNTY BOARD OF EDUCATION

Outstanding Achievement

IN

GRADE 13 French

SCHOOL YEAR 1983-1984

THE GREAT PLACES OF FRANCE

Texts by

PIERRE ALAIN

Translated by Evelyn Rossiter

LIBER

Inner leaf: the hill at Sion-Vaudémont, known as
« La Colline Inspirée » (Divine Hill).

Below: the village of Montignac-sur-Vézère, in
Dordogne, Périgord Noir (southernmost sector,
closer to the department of Lot-et-Garonne). The
Lascaux grottoes are located just above.

THE GREAT PLACES OF FRANCE

People have their roots in the land where they were born. They are often formed by that land, which guides them to achievements which shed light on their destiny. Others, driven by enthusiasm, find the purpose for work in a certain place. Strange bonds can be formed between the human being and nature, between people and their cities—bonds which, long after the deaths of those involved, leave a perpetually discernible mark wherever heroes had once been present, and wherever great events had taken place.

These are the *hauts-lieux* (Fr. "high places") where the spirit has been present or which once saw action which held great meaning for the culture. On the soil of France, which has given birth to so many ideas, such a wealth of art and a culture which has radiated throughout the world, these Great Places, as we shall call them, form an itinerary which encompasses history, art and science.

In these pages we have presented some of the most remarkable ones in France. They are to be found in all regions. They concern all disciplines, and they bring to mind the great figures who have made history or aided in the spread of knowledge.

Any choice is arbitrary, especially when the field is so rich! The places which we have decided to mention are intended to provide the broadest possible range in each sphere. We hope that our choice will take the reader on a journey through time—one whose stages will serve to illuminate the movement of ideas, in the places where they were expressed.

P.A.

Designed and Produced by
Productions Liber SA
© Productions Liber SA, Fribourg, 1982

Printed in Italy

ISBN 0-517-356171

AT THE DAWN OF MANKIND

The earliest great places of France lie buried deep in the mists of time, actually inside that land which has preserved until today a striking testimony to the lives of prehistoric men. In the south-western part of the country, in a lush valley situated between limestone cliffs—the Vézère—the remains which have been discovered are so numerous and so excellent that they made it possible for scientists to identify two periods: the first is that of Cro-Magnon Man, who was to be the prototype of the white races, and that of Magdalenian Man, from the last ice age, whose name derives from the Madeleine caves where the remains were found. Both of these sites are located near Les Eyzies, the French capital of prehistory. The carved flints and the bone and stone tools which were discovered there are evidence of the ingenuity with which man provided for his survival amidst hostile natural forces.

But the discovery of the caves in the late 19th century brought to light another phase, in which man first became aware of beauty and felt a need for ornament. The bracelets, pendants and, in particular, the chalk or charcoal drawings of local fauna on cave walls belong to this period.

The caves at Font-de-Gaume and Les Combarelles are decorated with pictures of bison, horses, reindeer and mammoths. Abbé Breuil of the Collège de France, has devoted his life to the

study of this prehistoric art. And it really is an art which commands our admiration with its keen reflection of reality and stylistic boldness.

In 1940 some children playing some distance upstream along the Vézère Valley stumbled across the Lascaux Cave, which was found to contain an extraordinary array of rock paintings, still in good condition, on the walls of a number of chambers. These ochre, red and black drawings depict bulls on the move and groups of horses, all portrayed with vivid realism.

Various theories have been put forward in an attempt to explain the meaning of these animal pictures. It seems likely that they were intended as a kind of magic spell by means of which the hunter hoped to bag his prey. In some of them, animals are shown transfixed by arrows in anticipation of the desired outcome.

The increasingly stylized nature of these works during subsequent periods confirms this symbolic function, just as female statuettes were thought to enhance fertility.

The Lascaux cave paintings could date from as early as 25 or 30,000 BC. Unfortunately, the deterioration of the paintings by exposure to outside air has made it necessary to close the caves to the public, at least until some solution has been found, in order to preserve this priceless treasure.

Above: one of the famous cave paintings in the Lascaux grottoes. Right: the Padirac abyss.

THE CARNAC MEGALITHS

Beyond the village of Carnac, where Saint Cornély watches over the flocks — (his effigy is on the church, surrounded by some cattle) — a landscape of gentle valleys stretches away into the hinterland. Morbihan, an ancient part of Brittany, has been a witness for thousands of years to a little-known civilization: the megaliths ("huge stones") embedded in the ground and reaching upwards to the sky, aligned on the points of the compass or solar trajectories. These crude monuments, which could have been moved only by a people endowed with considerable skill, are certainly of mystical origin. There are about 3,000 of them in the region of Carnac, though they do occur in other parts of Brittany. The rows of stones at Kerlescan, Kermario and Le Menec, closest to Carnac, are the most remarkable.

The mystical origin of the menhirs — "erected stones" — seems all the more plausible in that the Romans, after conquest of Gaul, adapted them to their own pagan gods, and the Christians later placed crosses on top of them, or carved symbols on their stone sides. The traditional use of the menhirs for religious purposes was thus adapted to changing circumtances.

The dolmen, which is also common in the area, is probably a funerary chamber formed of erected stones covered with a flat entablature. With the passage of time the dolmens have come to be exposed, though they must have originally been buried, like the *tumuli*, some of which can still be seen today: for example the Moustier Tumulus or the one at Saint-Michel, near Carnac, which was also Christianized.

Historians place the building of these megaliths somewhere between 2500 and 1500 BC. It is thought that they were the work of a people

of which little is known, but which certainly espoused certain spiritualist notions. Evidence of this fact is provided by the precise alignments and also by the cult of the dead conducted in the *tumuli*.

Stone alignment at Carnac, Morbihan. Opposite: a few of the megaliths.

The druids, who were the priests of the Gaulish and Celtic peoples, belong to a period later than that of the megaliths. The two cannot properly be associated, even if the great stone blocks were — as has been claimed — used by some druidic cult or other.

Like the rock carvings of Lascaux, in which natural elements were used for architectural purposes for the first time, the Carnac megaliths were erected at the dawn of man's intellectual awakening, at a time when his imagination felt the need for concrete expression and, from time to time, for enchantment or magic.

ALESIA, THE FRUIT OF DEFEAT

In the heart of Burgundy, between Auxerre and Dijon, between the valley of the Cure and that of the Haute-Seine, lies the small town of Alise-Sainte-Reine, in the shadow of the slopes of Mount Auxois.

Several centuries before the Christian era this was the site of the *oppidum* of Alesia, which underwent a memorable siege. At the western end of the plateau is a statue of Vercingetorix, which was erected in 1865 to commemorate the heroism of a man who can truly be said to be the first member of the French "resistance"!

At a time when rebellion was rampant among the tribes of Gaul under Roman rule, Vercingetorix, the young chief of the Arverni, succeeded in arousing genuine national sentiment among his followers. Overcoming regional rivalries, the "King of the Great Warriors" —the meaning of his name— urged the peoples of Gaul to unite and drive out the invader. An initial defeat at Gergovia did not dampen the ardor or the courage of the Gaulish leader, who then fell back to a position at Alesia, awaiting the support of his allies to break out of his encircled position.

However, help did not come. Despite their efforts, the besieged Gauls could not break out. In September 52 BC, after an atrocious two-month siege, Vercingetorix had to capitulate and personally surrender to the proconsul, in order to spare the lives of his surviving companions. He was then taken to Rome where he appeared in the "triumph" of Julius Caesar, among the trophies of his campaigns in Gaul. He was then imprisoned for six years and eventually strangled in his cell, on the orders of his captor.

By his heroism, Vercingetorix came to symbolize rebellion against foreign domination. He found in his defeat a well-merited glory. Alesia marked a turning point in the history of the young nation of France, as Celtic Gaul was succeeded by Roman Gaul. Of course, the invasion of the victorious legions also brought with it the benefits of Roman civilization and contact with the whole of the culture of Antiquity.

For many years nobody was quite sure where the siege of Alesia had actually taken place. In order to resolve the disputes among historians about this matter, Napoleon III ordered excavations in the area between 1862 and 1865. These brought to light the remnants of fortifications built by Caesar, together with human and animal bones, weapons, coins and other objects which were abandoned after the siege. The Alesia museum and the municipal museum, where these finds are on display, are certainly worth a visit.

Some distance from Alise, Sainte-Reine also reminds us of a Roman victory. Reine was a young woman who was executed in the third century for refusing to marry the Roman governor, Olibrius—whose name later became a French word meaning "braggart" or "swaggerer".

Above: statue of the Gaul general Vercingetorix in Alise-Sainte-Reine, in the Côte-d'Or region, and a glimpse of the village, featuring the site of Vercingetorix's Alesia stronghold. Opposite, to the right and the left: the fortifications restored to their state from before the Gauls' clash with the Romans.

NÎMES AND ROMAN FRANCE

Stendhal, in his *Mémoires d'un Touriste,* declared, while standing in front of the Maison Carrée in Nîmes, that he 'had seen nothing in Italy to match the 'pretty ancient style' of this remarkable work which, 'though laden with ornaments, was not lacking in genuine beauty'.

In a city richly endowed with Roman monuments—the Temple, the Roman Amphitheatre, the Thermal Baths and the Augustan Gate—the Maison Carrée has the charm of an art which, in other settings, tends to aspire to grandeur. An example of this is provided by the nearby Pont-du-Gard, a functional structure which has left future centuries with the boldness of its design and the beauty of a masterpiece which has withstood the ravages of time. Rome gave France a heritage whose ruins still amaze us today. The other sites which come to mind are those of Orange, Saint-Rémy, Fréjus, etc.

Above: the remains of the capital from a Roman column in the midst of Nîmes.

THE CITY OF CARCASSONNE

This fortified city stands on its rocky base like a vision from the Middle Ages. With jousting lists at the foot of the towers, and with its gateways and crenellated ramparts, its ducal castle and its basilica, this astonishing ensemble, which, though frequently rebuilt and restored, still retains a remarkable degree of unity, has a powerful effect on the imagination. During the first century BC, the Romans had made this city of the Narbonnaise a retrenched camp which withstood the barbarian onslaught until the fifth century. The Visigoths eventually took it and surrounded it with a second defensive wall which the Franks, however, did manage to penetrate three centuries later.

If we are to believe the troubadour's legend, it was during Charlemagne's siege of the city that Carcassonne came to acquire its present name. Carcas was the name of a woman who held power in the city. After five years of siege, Dame Carcas ordered the trumpets to sound the signal for the besieging forces to start negotiating. The heralds cried out "Carcas te sonne", whereupon the attackers repeated "Carcas sonne" to Charlemagne. And the name stuck.

The city later became a countship subordinate to Toulouse, and found its prosperity threatened during the Albigensian crusade. Simon de Montfort and 200,000 men from the north swept into Languedoc, the territory of those who were then considered to be heretics. After the sack of Beziers a new siege of Carcassonne started in 1209. The treachery of Montfort, who went back on his word by imprisoning the young Trenceval, who had come as an emissary, enabled him to take the city.

After the annexation of Roussillon in 1659, Carcasonne became militarily less significant than Perpignan. Construction had taken place at the foot of the rock, and the old city gradually fell into ruin during the next few centuries.

It was only in the mid-19th century that the writer Prosper Mérimée, who was at the time an Inspector of Fine Arts, alerted the authorities. The architect Viollet-le-Duc was dispatched to Carcassonne, with the result that, in 1844, the restoration work which was to last until quite recently finally got underway.

Organized visits are available, with qualified guides. In this way it is possible to form an overall impression of the defensive system of this forbidding fortress, to which access is provided by two gates: the Porte d'Aude and the Porte Narbonnaise. The castle, inside the city itself, is a bastion whose history can be traced all the way back to the 12th century. It now contains a museum.

As for the city ramparts, there is a fascinating account to be read in stone of the various construction phases, from the dry-wall technique of the Gallo-Roman era to the carefully chiseled pattern of the Monarchy.

The Saint Nazaere Basilica, with its eleventh-century nave, Gothic transept and altar area, the tombs of its bishops and statuary, is in itself a masterpiece of Southern art.

This—and the striking visual effect, the unusualness of the scene—combine to make Carcassonne an unforgettable experience.

Assorted views of the ancient city of Carcassonne.

VÉZELAY, BEACON OF THE WESTERN WORLD

Looking down over the old town, with its carved front doors and mullioned windows, the basilica of Sainte-Madeleine de Vézelay has withstood the ravages of the centuries and still affirms the glory of faith.

Its origins can be traced back to the ninth century, when a count of Burgundy, Girard de Roussillon, founded a convent at the foot of the mountains. In the 11th century the abbey was entrusted to the abbé of Cluny, whose prestige was then unrivalled in all of Christendom. The numerous miracles which followed the arrival of the relics of Saint Mary Magdalene attracted large crowds of pilgrims.

The Carolingian church was enlarged, but hill. The Norman invaders destroyed the building and expelled the nuns. Once the danger was past, the count established another religious house, this time a monastery, on the hill, and gave it to the

a terrible fire destroyed it on the eve of the great pilgrimage of 1120, burying more than a thousand pilgrims under the debris. The decision to rebuild was, however, taken immediately. The nave and the narthex were rebuilt, as well as a Gothic choir.

It was about this time, in 1146, that Saint Bernard, who, while at Cluny, had denounced the wealth and luxurious living conditions of certain prelates, went to Vézelay to issue an appeal for a new crusade. He had his listeners, who included the king of France, Louis VII, and numerous nobles, spellbound with his talk of recovering the tomb of Christ.

Vézelay's moments of greatness were not over: it was the scene of the meeting between Philippe-Auguste and King Richard Lionheart of England, who 50 years later was to direct the third Crusade, and also the site of the first monastery of the Minor Brothers of Saint Francis of Assisi on French soil.

Then it fell on hard times: during the wars of religion the Huguenots looted the abbey from top to bottom and the Revolution of 1789 also caused severe damage.

The fact that the building — which was made a basilica in 1920 — has recovered its initial splendor is due, as in the case of Carcassonne, to the vigilance of Prosper Mérimée and the genius of the young architect Viollet-le-Duc.

The façade was rebuilt according to the original plans, but the Romanesque nave, the transept and the Gothic choir are of the 12th and 13th centuries. The narthex, with its three sculpted portals and superbly ornate capitals is the only one of its kind in France.

Saint Bernard's plea for a crusade is marked by a cross on the Place de la Cordelle, where he actually preached. Yed the whole place — the castle terrace with its big trees, the view of the Cure Valley, the nearby village of Saint-Père and its church of Notre-Dame — together with its entire spiritual climate strikes one as the very embodiment of the sense of balance and moderation which are said to be the virtues of France.

The grounds and the Basilica at Vézelay. The cloisters and apse. The sculpting on one of the capitals.

THE CHANGING FORTUNES OF LES BAUX

A ghost-like town clinging to a rocky spur, in the heart of the Alpilles, Renaissance town-houses with sculpted façades, ogival vaults, a Saracen tower, chapels, the church and its lantern of the dead; an abandoned village where there was once a town of some 6,000 inhabitants. Mistral once described Les Baux as an "eagle's nest"—and its past certainly does include a number of noted predators!

A thousand years ago the domain was already powerful. The star of the Nativity which appears in its coat of arms was based on its lords' claim to be the descendants of Balthazar, one of the Three Wise Men. It held sway over several extortions so outraged the pope and the Count of Provence that they decided to hire mercenaries to subdue the man known as the "scourge of Provence". However, the mercenaries themselves proceeded to lay waste the countryside; Raymond de Turenne survived until 1400, when he drowned at Tarascon, while fleeing across the Rhône.

Even after his death, the region continued to be divided by intrigues and power struggles. On the death of Alex the city was incorporated into Provence as a mere barony. The second Queen Jeanne—Jeanne de Laval—received it from her husband, King René, and enjoyed living at the château. The fief then passed from hand to hand, life tenure being granted to loyal servants of the French crown. This was how the Connétable Anne de Montmorency received François I there in 1538. With the Manville family, its next occupant, the barony became a focal point of Protestantism.

Les Baux now offers a Romantic image of all that past greatness and of the subsequent decline—one which attracts vast numbers of visitors during the summer and also on Christmas Eve, when midnight mass is said in the old church of Saint-Vincent, in the presence of shepherds clad in their full cloaks, who come to offer a lamb at the service.

Various scenes from Baux-de-Provence. Below: Queen Jeanne's pavilion.

vassal villages, and alliances brought the lords of Les Baux some even more glorious titles, making them the Princes of Orange, Kings of Arles, and even Emperors of Constantinople.

The château was the brilliant setting for sagas of courtly love, attended by noble ladies and flattering troubadours. Towards the middle of the 13th century, a defensive coalition was formed, on the initiative of Barral des Baux, to protect the independence of the great cities against the ambitions of Charles d'Anjou. But, as one historian of the area put it: "Barral des Baux was such a coward that he treacherously sold to Charles d'Anjou the very Republic of Arles which had elected him to office at a time of common danger."

The tutor of the last princess, Alex des Baux, was her uncle, Viscount Raymond de Turenne, an odious character whose cruelty and

MONTSÉGUR, OR THE TRAGEDY OF INTOLERANCE

At the foot of the Pyrenees, perched like an eagle's nest on a rocky spur, at nearly 4,000 ft, the fortified castle of Montségur was the setting for a terrible tragedy of intolerance.

In the 11th century, a new religion originating in Asia reached Italy and the south of France. Based on Manicheism, or the theory of Manes (Manichee), it held that there were two opposite principles in creation: that of good, emanating from God, and that of evil, the work of Satan. One was the way of the spirit, and the other the dead weight of matter. Man was therefore required to tear himself away from his material self in order to be united with God through spirituality. Life was thus seen as a trial to be overcome in order to reach perfection. Hence the name *Cathares* ("the pure ones"), or The Perfect, which was given to the followers and the chosen ones of the Manichean faith. They were also known as Albigensians, as the influence of the sect had been particularly great in the region of Albi, and southwest France in general.

This heresy caused the most acute concern in papal circles. The assassination of the papal legate in 1208 unleashed a conflict which lasted several decades and soon took on the dimensions of a crusade, directed by Simon de Montfort. One of its consequences was the Inquisition, a ferociously intolerant institution whose influence lasted for centuries.

In Occitania, an army more than 300,000 strong eventually forced the Albigensians to surrender. But clandestine resistance was organized at the Montségur synod in 1232, and the implacable struggle went on for ten years or more.

The siege of Montségur, where some heretical deacons, more than a dozen knights and their aides, armed men and some fifty female members of the sect —including Esclarmonde de Foix, the owner of the land on which the castle stood— had taken refuge, began in May 1243. Using secret and extremely difficult steep paths unkown to outsiders, the defenders were able to remain in contact with the world beyond the siege and preserve their treasure. The site held by the Albigensians seemed truly impregnable; but

treachery eventually proved to be their undoing, and in March 1244 they were obliged to capitulate.

Clemency was promised to those who confessed their "faults" and renounced their faith. 210 of them preferred to die. On March, 16, 1244 a huge bonfire was built in a field at the foot of the rock, and the victims, headed by Esclarmonde, daughter of the lord of Montségur, her mother and grandmother, marched to their deaths.

Centuries later Montségur is still imposing and not too readily accessible. It takes more than an hour to walk up to the platform which towers over the cliffs from a height of more than 300 ft. The remains of the keep and a number of rooms are still discernible among the ruins. The strange manner of its construction suggests that the castle, built in 1206, was originally designed as a Manichean temple.

The castle-fortress of Montségur high atop the rock. Left: the village nestled below.

THE PALACE OF THE POPES, AVIGNON

Towering over the Rhône from the top of a rock which affords a commanding view of the valley, the Palace of the Popes in Avignon brings to mind a crucial period in the life of the Church in the early 14th century.

The death of Pope Boniface VIII, the failure of the Crusades and the conflicts between the cardinal Roman families had all severely upset the meetings of the Sacred College! The eventual outcome was the election of a French pope, Bertrand de Got, Archbishop of Bordeaux, who took the name of Clement V. With the support of Philip the Fair the new pope traveled to France and settled at Avignon, but it was his successor, Jean XXII, who, seeing that Italy was being torn apart by the rivalry between Guelphs and Ghibellines, truly moved the papacy to the banks of the Rhône.

The modest palace in which he lived was replaced under Benedict XII, in 1316, by a set of buildings comprising both palace and fortress, from which the surrounding countryside could be surveyed constantly.

Each of the popes of Avignon made additions to the buildings there. Urban V (1360-1370) laid out the ceremonial courtyard and built the east façade. When Gregory returned to Rome, the Palace had become truly a town within a town. The vice-legates who inherited it found in it a magnificent residence paved with marble, adorned with precious stained glass windows and with official reception rooms decorated by Giovanetti de Viterbo, who had painted frescoes on the walls.

Having become public property at the Revolution, the Palace was used for the sordid executions carried out by Jourdan Coupe-Têtes and Duprat the Elder. Under Napoléon it was turned into a barracks and was used for that purpose for nearly a century. During his journey in 1837, Stendhal drew attention to the results of that occupation: "The Palace is strangely ruined nowadays: it is being used as a barrack, and the soldiers have been peeling off the heads of Giotto's frescoes and selling them to the citizens of Avignon."

It was not until the beginning of the 20th century that the Palace, which had been donated to the State by the city of Avignon, was safe from vandals. Restoration lasted several decades. By 1939 the Palace had recovered its majestic appearance.

Overall view of Avignon and two close-ups of the Papal Palace.

THE FOUNTAIN OF VAUCLUSE, WHERE PETRARCH ONCE LIVED

The Fountain of Vaucluse is an unusual natural phenomenon—the resurgence of an underground river, the Sorgue, whose torrential waters come streaming out into a rocky amphitheatre. They then force their way through undergrowth and rocks, dividing into several branches before flowing through the small town of L'Isle-sur-Sorgue, which is sometimes known as the Venice of the Comtat.

The Fountain of Vaucluse is most famous, however, on account of Petrarch, who withdrew to this area in 1337, at the age of 33, to dream of his love for the beautiful Laura de Noves.

The poet had met her in the church of Sainte-Claire d'Avignon, on April 6, 1327. "There was something celestial about the way she walked," he wrote; "her stature was fine and light, her eyes tender and shining, and her golden hair floated over her shoulders, which were whiter than snow."

But the young woman was already married, and was too virtuous to yield to a guilty love. Despairing of ever winning her, Petrarch traveled to France, Germany and Italy, before returning to Vaucluse to celebrate the memory of her unattainable beauty. This ideal love filled his life and fed his literary creativity, as the only eternal love is that which never goes beyond the stage of desire.

The beautiful Laura died in 1348 from the plague which was then decimating the region. But the poet pursued his dialogue with her even beyond the grave: "Dreaming of love I sit and write:

She whom the heavens show and the earth now conceals,
I see and hear because she is still alive
And she still responds from afar to my mortal plaintive song:
Why have you been consumed before your time?
With pity in her voice she said to me:
Why shed these painful tears from your saddened eyes?
Do not weep for me because death has made
My days eternal; the eternal light
When they seemed closed suddenly opened my eyes once more."

Francesco Petrarch was often present at the pontifical court at Avignon. In 1341 he was given the poet's crown, at the Capitol in Rome. Then, tiring of his travels, he returned to his native country and settled in 1370 at Arqua, near Padua, with his illegitimate daughter Francesca.

The site of the Fountain will always retain the memory of this idealized love. Indeed Petrarch himself implied that he realized as much, when he wrote: "Already famous for its wonders, Vaucluse has become even more famous through my long stay there and through my poetry."

The ancient church and ruins of the Fontaine de Vaucluse Castle, to which Francesco Petrarca (Petrarch) retired following his blighted love for Laure de Noves. Opposite: column in the village center commemorating 500 years since the birth of the poet.

DOMRÉMY-LA-PUCELLE

This is the name of a village, on the border of Champagne and Lorraine, which a humble peasant girl made known throughout the length and breadth of France. She was born there in 1412. Her father had settled there two years previously and owned some 50 acres of fields and woods. The whole area was in a state of acute hardship as English forces roamed the countryside and armed bands held people up for ransom.

One day in the summer of 1424 Jehanne was leading her sheep out to graze on the hillside pastures of the Bois Chenu, deep in thought about the terrible times in which she lived, when suddenly she heard voices which seemed to be coming from inside the wood. The mysterious voices were announcing that she, a poor shepherd girl, had a mission to save the kingdom of France! She later realized that they must have belonged to Saints Michael, Margaret and Catherine, to whom she prayed frequently. For a long time she said nothing to anyone about this urgent appeal which she had heard. Four years later, Jehanne even-

tually confided in her friends the news of her conversation with the celestial spirits. And then, on May 13, 1428, having at long last decided to respond to the orders which she had received, she went to Vaucouleurs, to see Lord Robert de Baudricourt and ask him to help her visit the king, who had taken refuge in Chinon.

When confronted with this 16-year-old slip of a girl who sought to "kick the English out of France", Baudricourt burst out laughing and asked her escort to take her back home, with a spanking. Several months later, however, that same lord gave her an armed escort of six men for the journey. The reason for his change of heart was that, in the meantime, the young girl's fervor had convinced the inhabitants of Vaucouleurs. They had all contributed to the cost of fitting her out and buying her a horse. Then, dressed in a man's clothing and her hair cut short, Jehanne set out on February 23, 1429, to talk to the king of France. She was no longer a shepherdess; but, while not yet a saint, she was definitely a warrior driven onwards by her faith in her divinely ordained mission.

The miracle of Joan of Arc lay not in her celestial voices but in the events which were to mark her mission, right up to its fulfilment. Miracles have never taken as tangible a form as this; this one was the beginning of a saga whose sad outcome is all too well known. But the whole extraordinary venture began here, in Domrémy...

A peasant's house, four small rooms with a low ceiling and an attic overhead, and the young girl's room, dark and bare; in the garden there is a fountain with a bust of Jehanne, and, in the nearby church, the stone font where she was baptized...

A modest museum, founded by Pierre Marot in 1954, shows a number of documents and mementos. Some distance away, on a terrace adjoining the Bois Chenu, the basilica of Saint Joan of Arc still testifies to the glory of the girl who became a saint and a martyr.

The house where Joan of Arc was born in Domrémy. Above: frontispiece at the entrance.

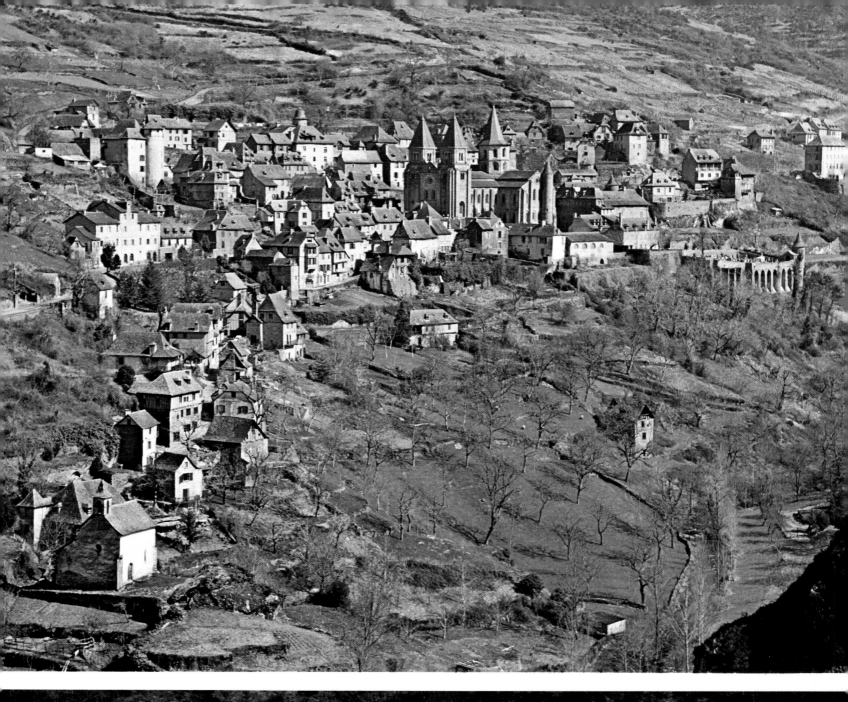

THE SAINTE-FOY BASILICA AT CONQUES

On the side of a narrow gorge, the ancient rooftops of the village of Conques huddle around the sandstone and black schist of the basilica—one of the finest and best-preserved samples of Romanesque architecture in France.

Since 866 the basilica has been dedicated to Saint Foy, a 12-year-old girl who was martyred in the third century by the Romans. Her remains were formerly at Agen, but the monks of Conques were anxious to ensure that the monastery, originally founded in the eighth century, should be honored by some relics capable of securing the divine favor, and, at the same time, attracting large crowds of pilgrims.

A first attempt to seize the relics of Saint Vincent in Spain was a failure. Then a monk from the Conques community had the bright idea of gaining admission to Agen and spending a few years there, waiting for the right moment to steal the relics of the young saint. He succeeded, having first earned the trust of his brothers in religion!

His return to Conques was triumphant. And the good saint, who was doubtless so deeply touched by such extreme loyalty that she must have been prepared to overlook the methods used to express it, responded by granting the desired miracles! The church was dedicated to her and her image, in an astonishing statue of almost oriental luxuriance still venerated by visitors to the basilica

Sainte-Foy is the patron saint of prisoners —as can seen from the captive's chains attached to the choir grill. The patronage of the saint has made the church one of the richest in France. For more than six centuries, the basilica has contained some remarkable vessels of precious metals, the reliquaries of Saint Foy and Pepin of Aquitaine together with a wide variety of donations.

Apart from this wealth, the basilica itself is an incomparable work of art. Because of its position on the pilgrim's road to Santiago de Compostela, it was predestined for greatness. Construction of the present building started in the 11th century and continued in the 12th, in keep-

ing with the purest traditions of Romanesque art.

With its three belltowers, its three naves, vast transept and the gallery on the side naves, as well as its abundant statuary, Conques certainly ranks as one of the most remarkable of the famous abbey churches, such as Solesmes, Cluny or Fontrevault.

The tympanum of the central portal depicts the Last Judgment. It is truly a fresco in stone, containing 101 figures, made with the vivacity but also the slightly crude workmanship characteristic of Romanesque sculpture.

The basilica of Conques is now run by the Premonstratensian Order.

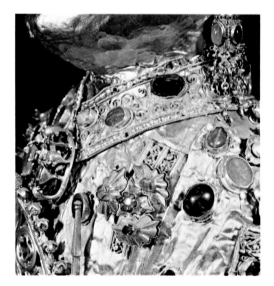

The village of Conques, in Aveyron, on the way to Saint-Jacques-de-Compostelle, and the basilica. Lintel of the portico and close-up of a decorated statue.

MONT-SAINT-MICHEL...
THE LEGEND BY THE SEA

A rock in the midst of the sand, a pyramid bristling with bell-towers, towering over the immense mud-flats which the tides relentlessly cover and uncover: a point which has remained fixed for centuries in an endlessly moving world. This outcrop of granite on the shifting sands is both a paradox and a symbol.

And it was only fitting that a legend — later to become history — should spring up here. Early in the eighth century, Bishop Aubert of Avranches had a vision of the Archangel Saint Michael, as he was meditating on Mont Tombe, as the rock was then called. An oratory was built and became an abbey in Carolingian times. Until the 16th century building proceeded apace, while the pilgrims came in large numbers in succeeding generations. Besides the faith, business also prospered. Shops selling souvenirs and fetishes to the crowds were set up at the foot of the rock; hostelries were established and a village thus came into being, while the Mount was becoming a sanctuary as well as a fortress.

Unwary pilgrims were occasionally cut off by the rising tide, which came in "at the speed of a galloping horse", or sank into the deceptively stable-looking sands. Mont-Saint-Michel was said to be "in peril from the sea".

Decline set in when the abbey, neglected by the monks, became a State prison during the monarchy: a kind of "provincial Bastille" in which the victims of the king's sealed orders were locked up. It served in this role during the Revolution and up to the 19th century; its inmates included the scholar Raspail, the revolutionaries Barbès and Blanqui. In a place of prayer, intolerance and horror also reigned.

In 1874 the abbey and its ramparts were taken over by the Department of Historical Monuments, and thus became part of the national architecturql heritage of France. And the Mount is truly a vivid display of building techniques over the ages: the Romanesque art of the first abbey with its supporting crypts, the ogival art of the Merveille (1211-1228) and the flamboyant style of the last Gothic period are all nobly represented here, in a beautiful natural setting.

Mont-Saint-Michel was an island at one time. Since 1881 it has been linked to the mainland by a raised causeway, the advisability of which was hotly debated and is still something of a contentious issue. If it had been left as an island there is no doubt that the crowds that now make it one of the most heavily visited sites in the whole of France would probably have stayed away.

Yet there is no place on earth which so sorely needs solitude and silence. These precious qualities can still be found, of course, after the flood of visitors has receded like a tide, and when the dream-like contours of the turrets and spires of the Mount stand starkly against the sea sky at dawn or dusk. Mont-Saint-Michel, a work of art, place of prayer and historical record all in one, is truly entitled to be regarded as one of the great places of France — one in which human science combined with the majesty of architecture to create a thing of supreme beauty.

Different views of Mont-Saint-Michel. Opposite, to the left: the inclined plane that made hoisting of construction blocks possible.

THE UNION OF BRITTANY AND FRANCE

In August 1532 the Parliament of Brittany, meeting in Vannes, solemnly proclaimed "the perpetual union of the country and duchy of Brittany with the kingdom of crown of France".

This proclamation confirmed the cession granted by the heir and daughter of Anne of Brittany, Claude de France, to her spouse François d'Angoulême who in 1515 became King François I of France.

Although Anne of Brittany, by marrying successively Charles VIII and Louis XII, had remained the sovereign of her duchy, the union was to be expected. The new province did, however, maintain some measure of autonomy: privileges were kept intact, as was jurisdiction over local affairs. There was still a Breton army, controlled and paid for by the duchy. On several occasions, for political and religious reasons, conflicts broke out with the central authorities.

Though Vannes was once the capital of the ephemeral kingdom of Brittany, Nantes and Rennes were also to vie for the metropolis standing, the latter of the two especially fiercely. Yet the first-named is the most reminiscent of Duchesse Anne by virtue of the beautiful castle there that still bears her name.

The castle of the Duchess Anne in Nantes. Right: the castle at Pau, birthplace of Henri the IV, and the sovereign bed chamber.

PAU: THE BIRTH OF THE VERT-GALANT

The Albret family was in power in Navarre when Margaret of Angoulême, the sister of François I, married Henri d'Albret in 1527. Jeanne Albret, their daughter, married Antoine de Bourbon, a descendant of Saint Louis. She followed her husband while he was off at the wars in Picardy against Charles V, and, when she was pregnant, waited until very close to her confinement before returning to Pau: after all, the heir simply had to be born in the castle of his ancestors. This meant crossing a large part of France in a wagon in the middle of winter! She reached the castle on December 3, 1553, and gave birth ten days later to a boy − as intended. Albret's grandfather greeted the baby and rubbed his lips with a clove of garlic and then a drop of Jurançon wine. Then he presented him to the crowd with the following words: "Here is the lion born of the lamb of Navarre!"

Such an entry into the world could only have been that of a striking figure of a man. And the young Henri did emerge from his childhood at the castle of Coarraze, near Pau, among the peasants, a truly warlike and impressive young man. At the age of 19 he married Marguerite de Valois, the famous Reine Margot, in Paris.

The castle of Pau, built in the 12th century on a rocky spur, before the blue outline of the Pyrenees, was turned into a sumptuous residence by the Albret family. Now it is a national museum. The royal apartments have been partly reconstructed.

Having conquered his kingdom, King Henri could say, flattering the pride of his fellow citizens: "I have given France to Béarn, and not Béarn to France."

CHARTRES, THE CATHEDRAL OF FRANCE

France is the land of the château, each of which has its own history. But it is perhaps even more the land of the cathedral. Each of them was born of the faith of the ordinary people and gave the usually anonymous architects and sculptors a way of expressing their genius in two art forms which, though commonly known as Romanesque and Gothic, should really be called by their more authentic titles: French and ogival art.

The first of these made its appearance in Burgundy, Auvergne and Saintonge. The second, which was born in Ile-de-France, with the humble churches of Val-d'Oise and Valois and the great cathedrals, whose architectural shapes followed the trends over the centuries.

Notre-Dame-de-Chartres, on the other hand, was destroyed by fire several times during its early history and rebuilt almost entirely in a span of thirty years, in its present form, between 1194 and 1225. It thus has a rather unusual unity of style: a Gothic which, though at the height of its development, still retains its initial vigor.

The "irreproachable spire which soars above all error", to use the words of Charles Péguy, rises like a prayer above the Beauce Plain, where the wheat fields undulate at harvest time. It is here, echoing the sentiments of the poet, that the Christian students of Paris come every year on foot to celebrate Whit Sunday.

Emile Male rightly perceived in Notre-Dame de Chartres "a visible expression of the thinking of the Middle Ages". It is remarkable for the majesty of its skyward thrust, with its two dissimilar towers, the fullness of its nave and the sculpted stone enclosure of the choir, while the wealth of statuary which adorns it is quite extraordinary.

Lastly, the magnificence of Chartres is completed by its 13th-century stained glass windows which, together with those of Bourges, are

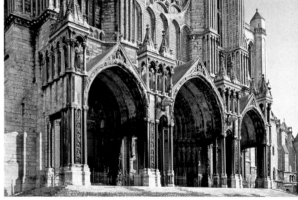

unique specimens of a long-lost art form. The sumptuousness of the colors is matched only by the imaginative treatment of scenes from the Old and New Testaments and the lives of the saints as well as the craft guilds of medieval Chartres, which also figure in the church's statuary. In this way the human and the sacred are mingled in an outpouring of popular faith.

When the sunlight plays on these transparent harmonies the effect is quite enchanting. Above all else, Notre-Dame de Chartres is, even for the non-believer, a temple of beauty.

The Cathedral at Chartres, its rose window, one of its noted stained glass windows, and vaults. The most visited place in all of France.

THE DOUAI BELFRY, A SYMBOL OF THE CITY

The Douai Belfry is the subject of one of the finest paintings of Corot's declining years— one in which the painter recovered the finesse and the mother-of-pearl brilliance of his youthful works.

The belfry is also a typical example of an architectural form peculiar to northern Europe, being found in Artois, Flanders (French and Belgian) and even the Netherlands.

The belfry is not a clocktower. It is the municipal building *par excellence*, as it symbolizes the freedom of the city in which it is located.

It is usually situated in the middle of the city, where it served as a watch-tower from which it was possible to scan the horizon. An alarm bell alerted the guard and could summon the populace to man the defenses.

The Douai Belfry, built in 1380 and fortunately spared by wars, is one of the most elegant of its kind, thanks to the corbelling of its turrets. At the top of its spire, 131 ft. above the ground there is a gilded copper lion holding in its claws the banner of Flanders. In July of each year, a bell weighing some 5 1/2 tons and a carillon of 49 bells celebrate the famous Fêtes de Gayant, the easy-going giant which is carried along the streets with its family of stuffed figures. This is an old Flemish tradition which is carried on in a number of northern towns.

The bell tower in Douai (14th-15th c.) with, below, its ceremonial staircase —the pride and joy of Flanders. Above and right: the Saint Sernin Basilica in Toulouse, one of the jewels of Roman art.

SAINT-SERNIN DE TOULOUSE, THE ROMANESQUE MARVEL

Toulouse is a great city which has figured prominently in the history of France.

In the heart of the "pink city", as it is called, stands the Romanesque cathedral of Saint-Sernin, with the lattice-work blind arches of its bell-tower, rising above the perfect Latin cross formed by its five naves and broad transept. No other Romanesque building can rival it for spaciousness and majesty. In the words of one author, "An entire profound past lives in this infinitely venerable church. Its choir is older than the first Crusade, and older than the Song of Roland. When the vaults of the sanctuary were built the Cid was still alive".

Toulouse stood at the crossroads of the great pilgrim routes to Santiago de Compostela. The monks who guarded the tomb of Saint Saturnin (or Sernin), the first bishop of Toulouse, decided to build a huge basilica to accomodate the crowds on their way to the distant Spanish shrine, as they rested before crossing the Pyrenees. Work started in 1080 and the choir was completed in 1096, being consecrated that same year by Pope Urban II who, together with Count Raymond, had come to prepare the first Crusade, amidst an assembly of bishops and lords.

The ornamental richness of the cathedral defies comparisons. More than 500 Romanesque capitals, a sculpted altar, the low-reliefs in the ambulatory, the famous tympanum of the Miégeville porch, with their human figures, imaginary monsters, beasts and stone flora form a genuine anthology of Romanesque art in stone.

A TEMPLE OF LEARNING:
THE SORBONNE

The Latin Quarter, so named because of its academic vocation, occupies a central place in French intellectual history. Since the Middle Ages, scholars and students have been busy dispensing and acquiring knowledge there. The Sorbonne is truly a temple of learning in which the greatest voices of erudition have been heard.

Its name derives from that of Robert de Sorbon, chaplain to Saint Louis, who founded it in the middle of the 13th century, on the orders of his sovereign. Its statues had been established in 1215 by Cardinal Robert de Courson, the legate of Pope Innocent III, by virtue of his religious powers. His intention had been to form a sort of college at which 'poor masters and students of theology, could receive both learning and hospitality.

The first printing press ever used in France was installed at the Sorbonne in 1470 — another great intellectual distinction. Cardinal de Riche-lieu had Lemercier reconstruct the buildings of the school between 1627 and 1642, and also replaced the old chapel by a new church which now contains the cardinal's tomb—a monumental work of sculpted marble — as well as a number of paintings, including some by Philippe de Champaigne. It is all that remains of the structures of the 17th century. A general reconstruction took place again between 1885 and 1901, in response to the needs of higher education in Paris, the center of which in Paris was now the Sorbonne.

Amphitheatres, reception rooms and lobbies are decorated with a profusion of paintings, unfortunately the work of the official artists of the late 19th century, whose pictorial efficiency was not matched by their talent. The Great Amphitheatre, which, with, 1,700 places, is the largest, does however contain the famous painting *The Sacred Wood,* by Puvis de Chavannes.

The church, which was built in 1635, has an elegant cupola. A portal with columns opens on to the splendid Cour d'Honneur, which provides a most suitable setting for outdoor concerts in summer.

During the student unrest of 1968 it was the headquarters of the dissident movement, where students and demonstrators held non-stop rallies. The Sorbonne, being a temple of learning, is also *ipso facto* a crucible of ideas, and consequently of student turbulence !

The small Place de la Sorbonne, facing the Boulevard Saint-Michel — or "Boul'Mich", as it is called locally — was recently cleared. Silvery linden-trees were planted near the statue of Auguste Comte, the founder of Positivism, who dreamt of a humanistic religion. While renovation was in progress a number of Merovingian structures were unearthed, thus testifying to the distant origins of this academic quarter.

The Sorbonne —(seen to the right: assorted views of the inner courtyard today)— was, for centuries, one of the most celebrated seats of knowledge in Europe.

LA DEVINIÈRE AND RABELAIS

A few miles from Chinon, where Jeanne la Lorraine identified her king in the midst of his courtiers, in the deeply historic Loire Valley, La Devinière consists of a group of farmhouses. In the middle of them is a 15th-century house, a dovecote whose outer staircase is adorned with a penthouse. François Rabelais, the son of a lawyer, was born in this humble abode in 1494. It was there that he spent his youth, which is the subject of a number of documents which have been assembled in a small museum.

All around is the countryside which he filled with his heroes and the villages which witnessed their adventures: Lerne, where the *fouaciers* used to go to sell their brioches at the Chinon market; Seuilly, which saw the beginning of the Picrocholine War described in Garantua in which the victor was Brother Jean des Entommeures, "bold, adventurous, cocksure, tall, lean, firm of mouth, haughty of nose, a quick dispatcher of the liturgical offices, a glib mouther of masses and a ready shirker of vigils—in other words, a real monk"; and La Roche Clermault, where the illustrious Grandgousier lived in the castle!

François Rabelais learned his prayers at the abbey of Saint-Pierre-de-Seuilly. Those gentle valleys and tranquil hills were seen by Rabelais through the medium of his imagination, together with the ruins and farmhouses which became the castles and fortresses of the giants who come to life in his works.

Edouard Herriot, a politician and astute man of letters, found Pantagruel 'a creed of the Renaissance' and Gargantua 'a contribution to the Reformation'. However, from the 17th and the 19th centuries, François Rabelais, in the words of Marcel Aymé, 'was to be, in the eyes of Frenchmen, nothing more than a funny writer who was also something of a nuisance, a Gothic barbarian trampling blithely on good taste and reason alike'.

« La Devinière », the house where Rabelais was born, in Touraine.

CHAMBORD...

The numerous superb residences which are to be found along the banks of the Loire make this valley a symbol of the greatness of the French monarchy in its prime.

During the Valois period, this valley was a favorite with the princes, who found in its delightful natural surroundings and well-stocked forests the pleasures of the hunt and of relaxation.

Louis XI was at Langeais, Charles VIII at Amboise, Louis XII at Blois and François I at Chambord. The latter is the largest of all the châteaux of the Loire, with 440 rooms, and has the most superb setting, with an estate of nearly 14,000 acres surrounded by a 20-mile wall — the longest in France.

Chambord was built by François I. On the site of the former residence of the counts of Blois, the king began construction in 1519, and pressed on relentlessly thereafter, despite financial obstacles. In order to pay for his project, he delayed the ransom which was required for the release of his two sons wxo were being held prisoner in Spain; he raided the treasures of the churches and the stocks of silver of his lords. But, twenty years later, in 1539, he was able to welcome his arch-rival, Charles V, to Chambord with the most lavish pomp, as young women clad in Greek tunics and little else strewed flowers before their imperial guest.

After it had been restored to the Counts of Blois, the estate became the property of the Crown once again under Louis XIV. Molière played *M. de Pourceaugnac* and *Le Bourgeois Gentilhomme* at Chambord for the Court.

The castle of Chambord with, right, Chenonceau : the most reknowned of the superb Loire castles.

...AND CHENONCEAU

If Chambord was the château of the kings, Chenonceau was certainly the domain of the ladies. indeed there is something feminine about its elegant architecture, spanning the Cher like a bridge. Its corner turrets and its long gallery seem to see their own reflections in the river, as if admiring their own beauty in a mirror!

It was a Tourangelle, Catherine Briçonnet, who, in the absence of her husband who was away with the army in the Milanais, supervised the building of the residence and its decor. This was in the year 1513. The owners died within two years of each other about 1525, and François I decided to scrutinize the estate's accounts, with the result that the unfortunate heir could do nothing but cede the château to the king.

Some 25 years later the château served as a gift again, this time to Diane de Poitiers, the favorite of Henri II. She set to work on the place with a true passion, laying out a garden along the bank of the Cher and building a bridge linking the château to the far bank of the river. The accidental death of Henri II cost her this cherished property. Catherine de Médicis, when she became regent, forced Diane to cede Chenonceau in exchange for Chambord, which she later aban-doned to spend her last days at Anet, another gift from the genorous Henri.

Chenonceau was further embellished with the twin-level gallery built on the bridge, which served as a princely setting for lavish parties, masked balls and other festivities, during which the guests were greeted by mermaids and by scantily clad nymphs emerging from the under-growth. Catherine's daughter-in-law, Louise de Lorraine, inherited the superb château, where she was to lead an austere widow's life, in a white mourning robe and a black-draped bedroom, after the assassination of her husband by the monk Jacques Clément.

NOTRE-DAME, THE SOUL OF PARIS

For the last eight centuries, the cathedral of Notre-Dame, located in the heart of what was once Lutèce and now is Paris, like a kernel inside its shell, has always been the soul of the city.

The site on which it stands was sacred even before Christianity had taken root. There is evidence of a pagan temple and of an initial 4th-century church dedicated to Saint Stephen, near which a cathedral of Notre-Dame mentioned by Gregory of Tours was built two centuries later.

In 1160 Bishop Maurice de Sully decided to replace the two structures by a more grandiose monumental building. Work started in 1163, on the basis of Sully's plans. Thereafter, each subse-

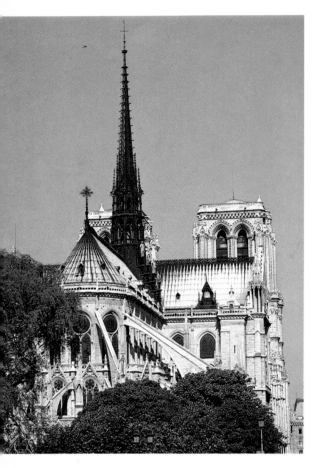

quent decade made its own addition to the fabric of the church; a succession of builders—Pierre de Montreuil, Pierre de Chelles, Jean Ravy and Raymond du Temple— had the cathedral finished by the end of the 14th century.

Vandalism then began. In keeping with a wish of Louis XIII, alterations were carried out which involved the destruction of the rood-screen, the high altar and the choir stalls. A century later, the canons had the walls whitewashed and replaced the stained glass by white window panes. During the Revolution the kings of Judah on the façade were smashed by the rioters, who obviously mistook them for kings of France! The cathedral was then dedicated to the Goddess of Reason. Admittedly, however, its sacred character was thereby implicitly acknowledged.

When it was reopened for worship in 1802 Notre-Dame was in imminent danger of ruin. The publication of Victor Hugo's novel, *Notre-Dame de Paris,* in 1831, eventually succeeded in drawing attention to the plight of a beautiful relic of the past which had withstood all attempts to destroy it. A decree was issued by Louis-Philippe in 1844, ordering restoration work which was entrusted to the architect Lassus. Viollet-le-Duc continued where he had left off in 1874, reconstructing the statues, erecting the spire and generally altering,

though only in order to save.

We are indebted to Viollet-le-Duc for this resurrection of a building which was so closely associated with the history of France and which was a landmark in the development of French religious architecture.

The annals of the cathedral make up a superb fresco of French history. Since the day in 1239 when a barefoot Saint Louis wore the crown of thorns in the central nave (his coffin was brought back to that same spot from Tunis ten years later), all the major national events have been echoed here: in 1447 a Te Deum for the liberation of Paris, under Charles VII; in 1594 Henri IV thanked God for the recovery of his capital city; in 1668, the marriage of Louis XIV, and, in 1804 Napoléon had himself crowned Emperor in the presence of the pope.

More recently, the funerals of some great men: Maurice Barrès, Foch, Joffre, Raymond Poincaré; Generals Leclerc, De Lattre de Tassigny; Paul Claudel and, on November 12, 1970, in the presence of numerous heads of state, the official funeral service for General de Gaulle, paralleling the private ceremony at Colombey-les-Deux-Eglises. More moving still was the ceremony of the Liberation of Paris, on August 26, 1944, the Te Deum of victory.

The Cathedral of Notre Dame in Paris: the most exquisite expression of ogival art and one of those monuments most steeped in history.

Of all the cathedrals which constitued the nobility of mediaval architecture in France, Reims has had the most glorious and also the most tragic history. It bears traces of its past on its burnt stonework, yet it also affirmed, by its solemn resurrection of July 1938, a creative determination to triumph over the worst disasters.

Fire destroyed the original church in the fifth century. But even that early structure already had its own history. It was here that Bishop Saint Rémi, on Christmas Day 496, baptized King Clovis, founder of the Frankish monarchy, who had been converted to the Christian faith by his wife Clotilde. The crypt and the baptistry of that first church can still be seen today. The first stone of the present cathedral was laid in 1211. One century later the nave and the choir were completed, in the full purity of the nascent Gothic style.

The towers had still not been completed when Joan of Arc, faithfully keeping her promise, led the Dauphin Charles VII, surrounded by his knights, to be crowned king of France in the new cathedral on July 17, 1429 — the day on which the French nation began a new life.

From then on, and symbolically in keeping with that rebirth, all the kings of France were consecrated at Reims — except Henri IV le Béarnais and Louis XVIII. The last one was Charles X, who was crowned at Reims on May 29, 1825.

The cathedral was not left unscathed by the turmoil of the Revolution. It was transformed into a club room and then a warehouse for fodder. Neither its architecture nor its statues, however, suffered as a result.

Reims was the cathedral of kings. And also, as André Michel pointed out, the cathedral of angels. They are everywhere, around the figure of Christ, near the martyred saints, on the walls of the apse, the vaults of the portals and along the pillars. An angelic weathervane stands on top of the spire, while the guardian angel of Saint Niçais has been dubbed the "smile of Reims". However, there are many other figures among the 18th-century statues of the cathedral which are illuminated with the same charming and graceful smile.

The 1914 war almost destroyed the building. Early in September it was hit by several shells. On September 19, the bombardment set fire to the scaffolding and the fire spread to the roof over the nave, destroying the beams and melting the lead in the roofs and the copper of the carillons. A few days later an 150 mm shell landed on the vault. Relentless shelling continued until 1918. A total of 287 shells hit the cathedral during the war.

Reconstruction started as soon as peace returned, under the supervision of Mr. Henri Deneux, chief architect of the Department of Historical Monuments, who devoted 23 years of his life to this seemingly impossible task. Almost half the funds were provided by gifts from John David Rockefeller.

The Cathedral at Reims where the kings of France were crowned. Left: the angel known as « Le sourire de Reims » (the smile of Reims), a national symbol. Right: the interior, and statue of Joan of Arc, whose odyssey culminated here.

VERSAILLES, THE RESIDENCE OF THE SUN KING

It took nearly a century, from 1624 to 1710, to turn Louis XIII's hunting lodge into a vast palatial domain with majestic buildings, terraces, ornamental ponds and finely manicured gardens, beyond the wrought-iron grill of the Place d'Armes. It is a composite masterpiece which, by virtue of its architectural design and the historical memories which it contains, symbolizes the lavish style of the *ancien régime*—and particularly the magnificence which earned King Louis XIV the epithet 'Sun King'!

There are a number of names which stand out in the history of the palace: Louis Le Vau, who fitted out and enriched the first building; Le Notre, who designed the French-style gardens; and later on Jules Hardouin-Mansart, who coordinated the entire set of buildings, was responsible for the apartments and the Galerie des Glaces, and built the famous royal stables, opposite the Cour d'Honneur, as well as the Grand Trianon (the Petit Trianon was built by Gabriel, under Louis XV), which combines charm with majesty.

While contemplating this magnificent architectural setting, one can readily visualize the solemn events which must have taken place at Versailles during the reign of the Sun King: lavish entertainment, including fancy—dress balls, courtly ballets, fireworks, which flattered the courtiers while impressing the ordinary people. The populace was not, however, excluded from the ceremonial goings-on, as can be seen from the records of contemporary witnesses. The Italian Primi Visconti wrote: 'It is a superb sight to see Louis XIV emerging with his bodyguards, in the midst of carriages, horses, valets and a host of people milling around noisily.'

Yet, curiously enough, it was not only on such occasions that the common man had a chance to see his sovereign. In the words of Restif de la Bretonne: 'Everyone in France regarded the king as a personal acquaintance.' When the royal family lived in the Louvre, the flow of visitors was so great that it must have been partly responsible for the decision to move out of town. Then, no sooner had the court settled in Versailles than a bus service was organized to take people to the palace. As Sebastian Mercier put it: 'Travelers would get off the bus at the gilded iron gates of the château, dust off their shoes, walk into the gallery and feast their eyes on the royal family.'

This refusal to seal himself off, even at the beginning of his reign, is thought to be due to Louis XIV's innate courtesy, the nobility of manner which makes the true greatness of kings.

Reigns and kings inevitably succeed one another. On May 5, 1789, the Assembly of the States General met at Versailles. It was during the meeting of June 20 that Mirabeau made his famous reply to King Louis XVI: "We are here by the will of the people, and it will take bayonets to make us leave!" On October 5, the Parisian mob went to Versailles, forced its way into the château and took the royal family back to Paris. The French Revolution had begun.

The lavish splendor and finery of Versailles — the pride and glory of the « Grand Siècle ».

SAINT-MALO, THE CORSAIRS' NEST

After the ravages of the second world war Saint-Malo has been admirably restored, with its stately ramparts and imposing stone mansions handsomely reflected in the water of its harbor. The proud statue of Surcouf, the most famous of its corsairs, stands symbolically facing out to sea.

Saint-Malo — named after Bishop Saint Maclou, who evangelized it in the sixth century — was most famous in the 16th and 18th centuries as a result of the audacity of its seafarers and its conquerors, whose frigates sailed the oceans.

Jacques Cartier crossed the Atlantic in the early part of the 16th century and discovered, beyond Newfoundland, an unknown land which he named Canada.

Duguay-Trouin, a real-life Romantic hero, was commander of a frigate at the age of 18; when taken prisoner by the English, he used his charm to win the favor of his jailer's daughter, thus regaining his liberty. He then went his corsair's way around the oceans of the world, from the Arctic to Brazil where, acting on instructions from the shipowners of Saint-Malo, he took Rio de Janeiro.

Surcouf was also an unscrupulous slave-trader who shipped Negroes to the New World in open defiance of the Convention. Eventually his amassed booty enabled him to retire, a rich and respected shipowner, in his native Saint-Malo.

Another distinguished figure associated with Saint-Malo — the poet and novelist Chateaubriand — who was also passionately in love with the sea, lies buried on an uninhabited island just offshore, beneath a granite cross.

THE PRISONERS OF THE CHÂTEAU D'IF

There are a number of islands in the Marseille roadstead, the smallest of them being the best known. The islet of If is occupied almost entirely by the castle of the same name which was built during the reign of François I, about 1530. For many years it was a State prison for political offenders, whose conditions of detention varied according to the gravity of their alleged crimes and also their social rank.

A dungeon dug out of the rock accomodated those sentenced to death. These included the victims of the riots of 1848 and 1851, who are commemorated on a plaque in the courtyard of the castle.

The much lighter cells — with a sea view! — situated around the second-floor gallery were occupied by high-ranking persons such as the unknown prisoner commonly referred to as the Man in the Iron Mask; Philippe-Egalite, father of Louis-Philippe; Mirabeau (imprisoned by his father for his debts); Lahorue, the Spanish consul in Bayonne: Prince Casimir of Poland and Mr. de Glandèves de Niozelles, who spent six years in prison for daring to appear in the presence of Louis XIV without first removing his hat!

The most famous of the occupants of the Château d'if were the heroes of the novel by Alexander Dumas: Abbé Faria and his young companion, Edmond Dantes, who became the Count of Monte-Cristo.

Left: the National Fort on the Bay of Saint Malo — a site venerated by such sea-faring adventurers as Jacques Cartier, Surcouf, and Duguay-Trouin. On the same page: the Castle of If, outside Marseille — as history will testify, one of France's most famous prisons.

STANISLAS SQUARE, NANCY

A Polish king in the ducal seat of Lorraine! The province and nearby Barrois were presented to the dethroned king, Stanislas Lecszinski, by his son-in-law Louis XV, who had married his daughter Marie. It was a gift for life only, however, and the duchy was to revert to France on the death of Stanislas. This family link was beneficial to the city of Nancy, the capital of the duchy, which the overthrown king governed for 28 years.

"In all the sections built by Stanislas, Nancy has kept that mannered grace which so well suited a courtly residence: a triumphal arch, statues and low-reliefs sculpted in the style of the period, groups of allegorical figures, pompous inscriptions which appear to be waiting for some absent master..." The historian Elysée Reclus described in these words the superb set of buildings of which it has been said that it constituted "perhaps the most complete and the most perfect achievement of 18th-century art". Two squares are linked by a triumphal arch: the Place de la Carrière and the Place Stanislas, the architecture around which was built between 1752 and 1760 from the plans of the architect Emmanuel Héré.

The splendid fountains of Amphitrite and Neptune, and a more recent statue of King Stanislas adorn the square. But its most beautiful adornment is unquestionably the series of wrought-iron grills, enhanced with gold, the work of Jean Lamour, together with the 45 wrought-iron balconies which decorate the sumptuous town hall and the other buildings of this unique gem of French architecture.

THE LEDOUX SALTWORKS
AND THE IDEAL CITY

Long neglected and generally ignored, the Ledoux Saltworks, at Arc-et-Senans in the Doubs, was rediscovered some decades ago. Its architecture now strikes us as the dream of a truly visionary builder!

Claude-Nicolas Ledoux, who was born in 1736, was one of the greatest architects of the 18th century. Well placed at the court of Louis XV, where he enjoyed the patronage of the Countess du Barry, he built a pavilion for the gracious lady at Louvecennes and showed his remarkable sense of grandeur in the famous stables at Versailles.

When commissioned to rebuild the saltworks at Arc-et-Senans, he designed a vast project comprising not only buildings for the treatment of rock salt, but an entire city, with a concentric layout, which was to be the ideal city. The venture was never completed, on account of the Revolution. His Saltworks, which were abandoned in 1890, were eventually taken over by the Department of Historical Monuments. They now stand as a kind of lesson in urban ideology, inspired by the mood of the Age of Enlightenment, but also ahead of their time as a model for the organization of capitalist labor.

Claude-Nicolas Ledoux was also the architect of Louis XVI. His other works include the Besançon Theatre, the prison at Aix-en-Provence and the famous gateways to Paris, long known as La Barrière...

**Left: the splendors afforded on Place Stanislas in Nancy, dating from a time when the Duchy of Lorraine "belonged" to a former Polish king.
On this page: two works of the master architect Ledoux in Arc-et-Senans—the visions of a luminary builder.**

THE MONTESQUIEU ESTATE
AT CHÂTEAU DE LA BRÈDE

Some twenty miles from Bordeaux, the Château de La Brède is an imposing stately home surrounded by moats. It was built in the 13th century, as was the keep, and has a 15th-century chapel. The estate had been presented as a dowry by Marie-Françoise de Pesnel, who was of English origin, when she married Jacques de Secondat, a former captain in the light cavalry. Their son, born in January 1689, was called Charles-Louis de Secondat, and later took the title and name Seigneur de Montesquieu, Baron de La Brède, when he was admitted to the bar at the Parliament of Bordeaux at the age of 19.

Eight years later his uncle, J.-B. de Secondat de Montesquieu, while on his deathbed, passed on his name to the young man, together with his post at the Parliament. That same year, Montesquieu was elected to the Academy of Bordeaux.

The author of the *Lettres Persanes,* published in 1721 and promptly banned by the monarchy, moved to Paris in 1722. However, he spent only a few months there each year, remaining faithful to his own region and his château, where he laid out a number of lawns and English-style gardens.

Reminiscent of two glorious moments in French letters: the Castle of La Brède in Gironde, with Montesquieu's chambers; and the domain of Ferney-Voltaire, straddling both France and Switzerland, with the bust of the writer gracing a village fountain.

Mr. DE VOLTAIRE,
THE SQUIRE OF FERNEY

In 1755, tiring of the harassment which he had to endure because of his writings—he had been a prisoner in the Bastille on two occasions—and failing to find the liberal spirit which he had hoped for in the king of Prussia, Voltaire settled in Switzerland, a Republican country, in order to escape the royal police in France. It was not long, however, before he became anathema to the Swiss pastors, who found his liberal philosophy repugnant.

Voltaire believed in a higher intelligence, responsible for the order of the "admirable machine" of the universe. But he denounced the sectarian bickering, and the despotism which, on behalf of that principle, the religions imposed on the consciences of men. André Maurois had this to say about his illustrious predecessor: 'Since it was impossible to be completely safe in either France or Switzerland, the wisest course was to have a foot in each country. With two houses on the lakefront and two along the border, he could, at the slightest sign of danger, flee until the storm had passed.'

After moving to the Château de Ferney, Voltaire was more severely critical than ever before of despots, tyranny and injustice. In the small world of Ferney he was also a 'model of the spirit of enterprise and of business sense which many heads of state and politicians might envy'. He could be chided, perhaps, for the pride he took in his property, and the ease with which he displayed his stud-farm, his livestock and farm vehicles; but he had a compelling way of conveying his strong personal ardor for reform and his passion for improvement.

THE MEMORY OF ROUSSEAU
AT ERMENONVILLE

North-east of Paris, to the south of Senlis, the Valois region is a place of forests and memories. The 'White Queen'—of Navarre—is associated with the Commelles Lagoons, Gerard de Nerval and *Sylvie* with the village of Loisy, Corot with Mortefontaine, and, above all, Jean-Jacques Rousseau with Ermenonville.

His tomb is situated here, though his body is in the Pantheon, where it was moved on the orders of the Convention in 1794.

In 1763 Marquis René de Girardin, one of the philosopher's disciples, having inherited the Ermenonville estate, decided to tranform this landscape of sand and swamps in accordance with the principles set forth in his book *Of the Composition of Landscapes and of Ways to Embellish Nature.* This was, to put it mildly, a presumptuous venture! He established an English-style park, adorned with a number of small symbolic structures and philosophical maxims carved on the stone-work, as an aid to meditation.

Fifteen years later he offered the use of the estate to Rousseau and moved him into a pavilion which has since been demolished. Unfortunately, the great philosopher did not have long to enjoy his tranquil retreat. Six weeks later, on July 3, 1778, he died suddenly. René de Girardin had him buried on the Ile des Peupliers, in the middle of the park—and it would doubtless have been better if he had been left there altogether. The park and the tomb have since become a center for emotional pilgrimages by the philosopher's admirers.

Ermenonville on the Ile-de-France: site of the last walks and the tomb of Jean-Jacques Rousseau. The tomb may be glimpsed on the islet, upper right.

Dom Pérignon was the procurator of his monastery, and in charge of the vineyards which, as early as the 17th century, made the area prosperous. He worked skilfully with his vines and found a process which would make the wine bubbly; he also wrote a *Memorandum* on the art of tending vines. Dom Pérignon, who died in 1715, was buried in the monastery church. By inventing this nectar of the gods, the reverent father brought fame and fortune to the region of Champagne.

From the vineyards where the light grapes are picked, the champagne eventually finds its way, via press, vat and bottle, to the cellars of the great houses which have been founded over the centuries, and whose prestigious names are a guarantee of their quality.

Emperor Napoleon visited these cellars in 1807. Today the 'route du Champagne' leads one through the vineyards and wine storehouses from La Montagne de Reims to the Côte des Blancs. The capital of the region is Epernay; it has a museum of the wines of Champagne, and, beneath the neighboring slopes, miles of tunnels hewn into the chalky soil, containing millions of bottles.

Patient and delicate supervision is required if the wine is to acquire all its marvellous properties. Periodically, each bottle has to be shaken by hand, and then the champagne decants slowly under the froth of years. Some *cuvées* are decades old. The records of the leading makers of champagne are museum pieces in their own right: it is possible to see in them Madame de Pompadour's orders and the order placed in 1952 for a special royal *cuvée* for the coronation of Queen Elizabeth II.

Not far from Epernay is the town of Ay, which has also been famous since ancient times. A song composed for the coronation of Charles VII mentioned its wine as the best in the region. Of course, in those days, Dom Pérignon had not worked his wonders, devising the uniquely wonderful drink which we enjoy today.

CHAMPAGNE, AMBASSADOR OF FRANCE

For centuries past, throughout the world, it has been a part of celebrations, both private and national. Its sparkle has added to the wit of many a dinner-party. Dom Pérignon, its inventor, certainly deserved the statue which was erected rather belatedly in his honor, in 1932, at Hautvillers, near the site of his abbey at Epernay, where all that remains now of the original structure is a fine portrait and one gallery of the cloister.

The vineyards of Champagne and the restored cell and wine cellars of the monk dom Perignon, who devised that technique that was to yield the world's most famed brew. Below: a roughly worked likeness of the monk winemaker in Hautvillers, where his abbey was to be found.

THE BASTILLE ONCE STOOD HERE

The Place de la Bastille is one of the historic sites in Paris. For the past 150 years the Colonne de Juillet, bearing a gilded bronze statue known as the Genius of Liberty, has stood in the middle of it. A circular white marble base contains the remains of the victims of the popular uprisings of 1830 and 1848.

All that remains of the Bastille itself is a few ruins from the counterscarp of the enormous military citadel after which the square was named. Built under Charles V in about 1370, the Bastille became a State prison under Richelieu, and in that capacity received such eminent guests as Bernard Palissy, Bassompierre, Foulquet, the Man in the Iron Mask, Latude, Voltaire and the Marquis de Sade.

In 1789 this symbol of the absolutism and tyranny of the old régime housed only a few forgers, two idiots and a small garrison commanded by Jourdan de Launay. On July 14, the parliamentary revolution developed into a riot. The insurgents went to the Bastille to demand weapons, and were received with a volley of rifle fire. The assault started at this point. Launay and his men were massacred, the few prisoners were released and the Bastille was occupied. Being the image of the hated régime which was to be overthrown, it was razed the next year.

It was not until 1880 that the date of the taking of the Bastille became the National Day of France, commemorating a new era of liberty.

Two reminders of a Revolution whose principles were to sweep the world: the column in Paris commemorating the Bastille and Strasbourg, as it appeared to the author of « La Marseillaise ». Right: the official plaque marking the house where the anthem resounded for the first time. Also, Rude's celebrated bas-relief on the Arc-de Triomphe in Paris, sculpted to capture the same Marseillaise spirit.

THE BIRTH OF "THE MARSEILLAISE" AT STRASBOURG

On August 1792, the mayor of Strasbourg, Frédéric de Dietrich, invited a number of officers from the garrison to dinner. War had been declared on Austria the day before and the guests, who included a young captain, Rouget de Lisle, who was also a poet and musician, were in a highly patriotic mood. The mayor asked his young guest to write a song which would lead the French troops to victory.

In a single night, Rouget de Lisle wrote the words and music of a song which he performed himself the next day, in the company of Dietrich and his friends. It was received with great enthusiasm.

The Marching Song of the Army of the Rhine was immediately published in Strasbourg and sent to all the volunteer forces converging on the capital. The troops from Marseille were the first to sing this song in Paris, so it naturally came to be known as the *Chant des Marseillais,* and later as *La Marseillaise.*

As its patriotism was blended with revolutionary sentiments, the *Marseillaise* was banned during the Second Empire, and was virtually forgotten fifteen years after it had been written! Paradoxically, it was next played to Parisian ears by an Austrian band, at a concert in the Tuileries in 1867. It was a true resurrection!

In the meantime the song had been adopted by the revolutionary movements of Europe in the middle of the 19th century, particularly by the Italian *Carbonari.* In foreign countries it has

remained a symbol of liberation. In another paradox, this vengeful and aggressive marching song became a national anthem—a purpose for which it was not at all intended!

Another curious effect of circumstances was that the house—since demolished—at 3, Place de Broglie at Strasbourg, where it was heard for the first time, was also the birthplace, in 1858, of a child destined to be an apostle of peace: Father Charles de Foucauld.

THE TEMPLES OF NATURE

As Maurice Barrès once put it, "There are places where the breath of the spirit blows". That spirit can express itself through the thinking of philosophers, the pen of poets and the brush of painters. One finds oneself saying, on first seeing a particular landscape: "It's a real Corot!" After seeing Cézanne's paintings so often, one begins to perceive only *his* colors in the actual landscape of Provence!

Although man can impose his view on things, there are also places whose fierce grandeur, delicate charm or well-preserved nobility can delight the human mind quite as fully as any work of art. There are many such places in France, because of the diversity of the French landscape. The "French climate" consists of nuances as subtle as those on which the artist must rely. Plains, mountains, rivers, oceans all command the admiration of the visitor. There is truly a "breath of the spirit" in these places which conveys its message to those sensitive enough to receive it.

How is one to choose from a such a disconcerting abundance? Let us try to place a few markers here and there on the hexagon which forms the link between the Nordic and the Latin worlds, between the northern plains and the stony, sun-drenched hills of the Mediterranean—an area bordered by seas which seem to belong to entirely different continents, from the cold, misty North Sea to the brilliant blue of the Mediterranean.

This spirit of nature is a breath of divine life, in places which inspire faith and fervor. During the furious equinoctial thunderstorms at the Pointe du Raz, one can imagine one is hearing the Voice of Eternity. This same spirit accounts for the numerous legends which have come into being in Brittany, whose rocky shores, perched at

The more hallowed sites in a nation often include the grandiose or exceptionally characteristic works of nature. Certainly, no other country can lay claim to such an infinite variety as France: here the Cape at Raz, where the coast of Brittany juts out at its furthest point, or Mont Saint Odile in Alsace, the Verdon gorges, or the shores of the Baie des Anges combine the snow of mountain caps with the rippled surface of the Mediterranean.

the tip of Europe, have been so battered by the ocean.

Other legends are born in quieter, even more secret places. Sainte-Odile, on a mountain slope in the Vosges, is surrounded by a strange megalithic wall six miles long. Here, more than thirteen centuries ago, a young girl who had been driven out by her father, longed to devote her life to God, and founded the first convent in Alsace.

Why is the harmonious curve of the shore near Nice known as the Baie des Anges, if not because the beauty of its natural setting and the gentleness of its climate both suggest the idea of Paradise?

Natural beauty can also be harsh and wild, in the Verdon Gorges, the effect of some distant cataclysm in the Provençal Alps; on the slopes of Mont Blanc, where huge rivers of ice flow all the way down to the valley below; or on the mountains of Auvergne, with their petrified craters formed in some primeval geological upheaval.

There are other places, of similar stature, where man and nature meet—towns where the faithful image and secret charm of the past have been well preserved.

Such is La Rochelle, with its towers, Honfleur and its ancient rooftops, Sarlat, and so many others that one simply comes across quite by chance while traveling through France! Places like the Camargue, with its horses and its birds, and Corsica, where the red cliffs of Piana are a sight to behold!

...Other cherished sites in France: Mont Blanc, the highest point in Europe, a seaport on the West coast (La Rochelle), an old farm in ancient Auvergne, Camargue, and the beauty of the bay at Piana in Corsica.

FONTAINEBLEAU :
SPLENDOR AND FAREWELL

Originally there was a fortress, to which King Louis VII added a chapel which was consecrated in 1169 by Thomas Beckett, at the time a refugee in France. The buildings were enlarged by Saint Louis. Philip the Fair died there. Charles V, in 1363, founded the library, the contents of which later formed the core of the Bibliothèque Nationale.

The true founder of the palace of Fontainebleau was François I, who brought in a number of great Renaissance artists to complete the decor: Primatrice, Rosso, Vignole, etc. The School of Fontainebleau was their creation.

The expansion and embellishment of the château was continued by the successors of François I: Henri II, seeking to please Diane de Poitiers, and then Henri IV who spent a fortune on it. Louis XIII was born in the palace and Louis XIV spent several months there each year.

The palace had already seen some moments of greatness: in January 1564 Catherine de Médicis, escorted by fifty maids of honor, had received the ambassadors of the pope, the emperor and the king of Spain. During the reign of Louis XIV, princes and kings were housed there. Louis XV tended to live elsewhere, but

Louis XVI was fond of hunting in the forest, in the company of Marie-Antoinette.

During the Revolution the palace was used as a prison. Napoléon, as soon as he came to power, started restoring it. When he greeted Pope Pius VII, who had come on his request to crown him emperor, in 1804, it was a clearing on the Fontainebleau estate—and Napoléon was wearing hunting clothes. Eight years later the sovereign pontiff returned to Fontainebleau as a captive and stayed there until the Concordat put an end—at least for a time—to his temporal power.

The Red Salon of the emperor's private apartments was where he signed the instrument of his abdication, on April 5, 1814. Two weeks later he assembled the veterans of his old guard in the ceremonial courtyard for the sad farewells which have become popularized in legend.

His spectacular farewell was, in actual fact, only an "au revoir"! One hundred days later, dismissing his failure, Napoléon returned from

The castle of Fontainebleau, where one is especially mindful of Napoleon's leave-taking: at the lower left, the Emperor's chambers; above, the staircase and court « des adieux » (farewells); opposite, the lane down which Napoleon was to vanish forevermore.

the island of Elba, landed at Golfe-Juan and made his way to Paris. Yet in fact he was merely consummating his defeat and leaving France to the invaders.

Today it provides its international visitors with a picture of ages gone by. Ceremonial courtyards surround buildings, beyond which stretches the garden of Diane, with its fountain

and its vegetation. The magnificent interior decoration of the palace has been preserved. With its Gobelins and Beauvais tapestries, its collections of porcelain adorned with the royal coat of arms, a Chinese and Indo-Chinese museum, and numerous paintings and sculptures, the Château of Fontainebleau is an outstanding art gallery in its own right.

THE ARC DE TRIOMPHE AT THE ETOILE

The greatness of a monument is due not only to its architectural merits, but also, and perhaps primarily, to its physical location. That of the Arc de Triomphe in Paris is exemplary. At the top of what was once Roule Hill, this structure is at the heart of a star radiating along twelve straight avenues, the most famous of which, at right angles to the main façade, is the Avenue des Champs-Elysees. The majestic setting of the arch is best judged from the upper platform. Rarely has a piece of architecture dominated its surroundings so completely as this.

The idea for a triumphal arch originally occurred to Napoléon, who mentioned it in a letter to Champagny on February 18, 1806. The site was chosen in May and plans were drawn up by the architect Chalgrin. The first stone was laid on August 15 of that same year. Progress in building it was curiously slow. By the time Napoleon had been ousted, the arch had still reached a height of only 16 to 19 feet above ground. Work then stopped altogether for a while, and was resumed only in 1825, and completed in 1836, under Louis-Philippe.

Empires sometimes survive a shorter time than men, and collapse with the monuments erected in their honor. Napoleon's intention was

probably to commemorate the victories of the Revolution and those of the Empire. They are depicted in the high reliefs which adorn the structure—including the superb *Départ de 1792*—popularly known as *La Marseillaise*—by Rude, and, on the opposite face, *Le Triomphe de 1810,* by Cortot.

The true significance of the arch was not fully expressed until a century later, when the victory parade after the First World War was held on July 14, 1919.

It had previously celebrated posthumous glories: four years after its completion, on December 1840, Napoleon's ashes passed beneath it on their way from Saint Helena to Les Invalides, and on May 22, 1885, it was also part of the setting for the funeral of Victor Hugo.

In this way the Arc de Triomphe has always had an air of funereal solemnity about it—precisely the reason why it was chosen as the site for the Tomb of the Unkown Soldier, who was buried beneath a bronze-rimmed slab on November 11, 1920, two years after the victorious armistice which his sacrifice had helped achieve.

Since then the flame which burns over the tomb has become a symbol of patriotism; in the same spirit, the mortal remains of victorious generals were placed for one day under the Arc de Triomphe: Foch, on March 24, 1929; Joffre, January 1931; Leclerc, December 1947, and De Lattre de Tassigny, January 15, 1952.

The Arc de Triomphe and the Avenue des Champs-Elysees are still the setting for victory parades and national commemorations.

The Arc-de-Triomphe at the Etoile and the Tomb of the Unkown Soldier — the nation's leading monuments.

THE HOTEL DES INVALIDES AND THE EMPEROR'S TOMB

The Institution des Invalides was founded in May 1670, during the reign of Louis XIV. Its purpose was to provide a home for the surviving victims of the wars which marred the reign of the Sun-King. The architect Liberal Bruant was commissioned to design the building. Within no time at all there were between 5,000 and 7,000 persons living there at the State's expense. The institution was headed by a governor.

A church was built behind the main buildings, and construction was continued by Jules Hardouin-Mansart, who crowned the structure with the majestic dome which towers over the esplanade.

Over the centuries the Hotel des Invalides lost its rather monastic air. However, there were still veterans living in it as late as the 19th century. Despite its huge size, of course, it would have been grossly inadequate to accomodate the victims of the holocausts of the 20th century!

Les Invalides now houses the Musée de l'Armee, a number of services of the Ministry of Defense, while the Church of Saint Louis has become the burial place of the marshals of the Empire and of a number of eminent soldiers, from Turenne to Marshal Foch.

In this way it is the Pantheon of the military glory of France. There are statues and mementoes wherever one turns, in the museum, the gardens and the formal courtyard: one of the famous "taxis of the Marne" which took soldiers from Paris to the front line in September 1914; guns from various periods; a tracked vehicle used in the first crossing of the Sahara by car in 1922-23, and the hearse which transported Napoleon's body to Saint Helena as well as the copper sarcophagus which carried the Emperor's ashes.

The monumental tomb of Napoleon I, of red Finnish granite on a base of green Vosges granite, is situated inside the church. Twelve colossal figures depicting the principal victories of the Emperor's reign stand facing the tomb. 53 flags captured at Austerlitz are grouped together in six trophies.

A reliquary situated in front of Simart's statue of the Emperor contains the sword from Austerlitz, the hat worn by Napoleon by Eylau, and the great necklace of the famous Legion of Honor.

L'Hôtel des Invalides (originally the Veterans' Hospital), erected in praise of French military exploits, where the Saint Louis Chapel houses the tomb of Napoleon (below). A huge and grandiose concourse sets it apart from the Alexander III bridge (above).

SACHE WHERE BALZAC LIVED

Saché: a chateau in the midst of a park on the banks of the Indre, in the heart of Touraine, where the author was born. A valley which Balzac compared to "a magnificent emerald bowl, at the bottom of which the Indre winds its serpentine way". And he added: "If you want to see nature in its full beauty, as virginal as a young maiden, go there one day in spring, and you will see love beating its wings against the huge sky."

It was in this valley that the author of the *Comédie Humaine* placed the action of his novel *Le Lys dans la Vallée,* and it was in this chateau that he wrote part of it, depicting in his Madame de Mortsauf the memory of his first love.

The 16th-century Chateau de Saché then belonged to Mr. de Margonne, a friend of the Balzac family. The novelist's study, which is open to the public, has been left as it was when he was alive, with an armchair at the desk where he did his writing and a bed in the alcove. Other rooms contain manuscripts, portraits and original editions from the period. The drawing room on the first floor still has its original furniture and tapestries.

A number of important works were written at Saché, where Balzac stayed frequently: *Louis Lambert,* the hero of which had been a fellow-pupil at the Collège de Vendôme, *La Recherche de l'Absolu* and *Le Père Goriot.*

"Don't ask me why I like Touraine", said the author; "my feelings about it are not the fondness one has for one's cradle, nor for an oasis in the desert: in fact I like it just as an artist likes art... Without Touraine, my life could even come to an end."

Besides his roots in Touraine, Balzac was also a Parisian. The house where he had his printing press is still standing in the Latin Quarter, in Rue Visconti. But his memory is more particularly present at Passy, in his house at 47, Rue Raynouard, with its garden facing the narrow Rue Berton, which has changed little in the past century.

His house has since been made into a museum. It had been built in 1753 as the servants' quarters of a mansion which was eventually demolished. Numerous documents recall the events of Balzac's life and career, which was so often difficult: they include letters, manuscripts, portraits of him and his friends, caricatures by Daumier and Granville, pages from his works and printer's proofs, heavily laden with corrections, letters to his publishers, etc.

The vine in the garden has been allowed to grow wild again. In the Rue Berton, facing the garden gate, a sandstone marker bears the inscription: "This boundary stone was placed here in 1731 to indicate the limits of the domains of Auteuil and Passy."

Saché, in Touraine, is where one is most keenly put in mind of Balzac — firstly, because it was he who resided in this fine manor house (below: his bedroom), and, secondly, because he was native to the region and thoroughly enthralled by his homeland.

THE VICTOR HUGO MUSEUM
AND THE PLACE DES VOSGES

The Place des Vosges, formerly known as the Place Royale, with its Louis XIII galleries and buildings of brick and stone, is one of the most harmonious in Paris.

Victor Hugo lived in one of the arcaded town houses, the Hôtel de Rohan-Guéménée, from 1831 to 1848. As a result of the famous Bataille d'Hernani, at which conservatives had fought his supporters at the premiere of his new play, he had become something of a public figure.

He had the standing of the leader of a literary school, and as such was visited by numerous friends at Place Royale.

The events of 1848 and the election of the president-prince totally altered the poet's political thinking. Having been elected as a deputy to the Constitutive Assembly he denounced the candidate's ambitious designs. Three years later the coup d'état of Napoleon III took place, and Victor Hugo was forced into exile.

The Hotel de Rohan-Guéménée was donated to the City of Paris by Paul Meurice, the poet's executor, so that a museum should be established in his name. Furniture designed by Victor Hugo for Juliette Drouet's house on Guernesey have been assembled in the third floor apartment where Hugo lived. His former study has been altered in connection with the reconstruction of his funeral chamber on the Avenue d'Eylau.

Victor Hugo, the most prolific and lyrical of French poets, was for a long while resident of this building on Paris's very lovely Place des Vosges (far right).

BERLIOZ'S HOUSE
AT LA CÔTE SAINT-ANDRÉ

La Côte Saint-André, a small town in the foothills of the Alps, is the birthplace of Hector Berlioz, the Romantic musician who, after early difficulties, triumphed in Europe towards the middle of the 19th century.

Though his family would clearly have preferred him to go into medicine, Berlioz eventually managed to convince his father to let him follow his musical vocation. The decision was actually taken in the study of Dr. Berlioz, which still contains the original family furniture.

The room in which he was born is on the second floor, where the young composer's diplomas (the Prix de Rome at the age of 27) are on display, together with the instruments which he played throughout his childhood: flageolet, clarinet and guitar. Hector Berlioz spent the first eighteen years of his life in this house, and returned to it frequently until his father's death.

La Côte Saint-André also promoted the renown of its son by organizing, in connection with the opening of the museum in 1935, a performance of *The Damnation of Faust,* in the great rafftered 16th-century hall. In 1969 other performances commemorated the century of his death.

The remains of another great artist, the Dutch painter J.-B. Jongkind, a contemporary of Berlioz who was one of the precursors of impressionism, lies buried in the cemetery of La Côte Saint-André.

Berlioz, doubtless the country's greatest composer, was born in Côte-Saint-André, in the Isère region. Seen below, Berlioz's house, which has since been converted into a museum.

THREE CENTURIES OF DRAMA:
THE COMÉDIE FRANÇAISE

In 1980 the Comédie Française celebrated its three-hundredth anniversary. In 1680 Louis XIV issued a decree requiring the three theatrical troupes then existing in Paris—those at the Hôtel de Bourgogne, the Theatre Guénegaud and the Marais—to unite and form the troupe to be known as Les Comédiens du Roi, which in 1689 was called the Comédie Française.

Neither Molière nor Racine, who died in 1673 and 1684 respectively, and whose works have figured prominently in its repertoire for the past three hundred years, were ever performed by the famous company during their lifetimes. In those days it performed on a stage in the Rue des Fossés-Saint-Germain, at the site of the modern 14, rue de l'Ancienne-Comédie and 17 and 19, rue Grégoire-de-Tours, where traces of the basements

and the theatrical property store still subsist.

In 1782 the company, directed by the great actor Talma, moved into the hall of the present Odéon, while construction was beginning at the Place Royale, from plans drawn up by the architect Victor Louis. At the south corner of the galleries, the Théâtre-Français was built from 1786 to 1790, after which part of the company performed there.

After the Revolution, the Comédie-Française was renamed Théâtre de la Nation. In subsequent years its actors frequently ran afoul of the new regime, which regarded it as a bastion of royalism.

During the night of 3/4 September 1793 all the actors of the company were arrested, and Collot d'Herbois delivered his famous denunciation in which he observed: "The head of the Comédie-Française will be guillotined and the other members deported."

The actors were saved only as a result of the dedication of a member of the Comité du Salut Public (Committee for the Public Good), who managed to remove damaging evidence from the files. After this narrow escape the actors took

the title of Théâtre de la République.

When Napoléon came to power the survival of the group was assured. Its organization was placed on a definitive basis in the famous Moscow Decree of 1812: it was to be a society directed by an administrator appointed by the government and receiving a national subsidy. In 1799 the Théâtre de la Place Royale had taken the name of Théâtre-Français.

The company's prestige constantly grew not only in France but throughout Europe, ever since the day when Talma, after a performance in Dresden, during the Empire, had declared: "We have played to an audience of kings."

In the 19th century and since, the stage of the Théâtre-Français has been a perfect home to the classical repertoire and to some remarkable theatrical events. The Bataille d'Hernani in 1830 brought traditionalists and Romantics to blows at the first performance of Victor Hugo's drama of that name. For playwrights and actors alike, the stage of the Théâtre-Français equals official acceptance—in other words, by the standards of our civilization, immortality!

La Comédie-Française, foremost among the world's theatres for three centuries. Left: a bust of Molière and the grand staircase. Above: the ceiling of the theatre hall proper. Below: a theatre lounge.

THE LOUVRE OF KINGS
AND THE LOUVRE OF THE ARTS

The Louvre, one of the biggest and best endowed museums in the world, is a household word for art lovers everywhere.

It started life as a square chateau, built during the reign of Philippe-Auguste, on the bank of the Seine, was expanded over the centuries and eventually abandoned when the kings of France moved to the Loire Valley. Around 1530, François I decided to return to Paris; he demolished the keep and the towers and built a palace to match the stately homes of Touraine and Valois. Pierre Lescot was commissioned to take charge of the project. The king died, and his successors were the ones who enjoyed the newly completed Louvre.

Catherine de Médicis and later Henri IV carried on the work of construction and embellishment. Each reign and each century added a wing, a courtyard or a gallery to the building. The palace became increasingly residential, with a theatre, library and art gallery. In this way when the court moved to Versailles, the Louvre was already destined for an essentially cultural future.

François I also founded the royal collection of works of art which was the basis for the treasures now owned by the museum. On the death of the king, the collection already included some great masterpieces; in particular, six paintings by Raphael, four by Leonardo da Vinci and Titian's portrait of François I. It was also to expand with the passage of time. The museum was actually set up by the National Assembly of 1792. Two years later its rooms were opened to the public.

The Napoleonic campaigns made it possible—by means of treaties imposed on the vanquished—to acquire numerous works which were then moved to the Louvre and exhibited there. After the fall of the Empire, the treaties of 1815 returned most of this booty to the countries from which it had been taken.

Even so, the Louvre is staggeringly rich! It encompasses every form of art: painting, drawing, sculpture, furniture, precious metals, etc., from every conceivable source and period. Egyptian, Greek and Roman antiquity is particulary well represented.

Beyond the Mollien and Denon galleries, which are lined with sarcophagi, the statue known as the Victory of Samothrace towers over the great staircase leading to the upstairs painting galleries. It was discovered at Samothrace in 1863 by a French expedition.

The most famous ancient statue in the Louvre, besides the Egyptian *Crouching Scribe,* is the *Venus of Milo,* a Greek masterpiece which was found on the island of Milo in 1820. It was bought by the French ambassador in Constantinople who donated it to King Louis XVIII.

The fame of the Venus of Milo is matched only by that of *La Gioconda,* by Leonardo da Vinci, a portrait of Mona Lisa painted in Florence around 1505, apparently after some four years of intermittent thought and effort. It was stolen in 1911 and recovered two years later in Italy.

A collection of views of the Louvre. Below: visitors crowding on to the grand staircase.

THE "ROYAL CROWN" OF CHATEAUX

They surround Paris like a crown of sculpted stone which tells the story of the evolution of styles from the splendors of the Renaissance to the classical French art of the 17th century. Together with the forests, they are the unquestionable appeal of Ile-de-France; they are, as it were, lighthouses along its shores, illuminating the past.

Vincennes, one of the favorite residences of the kings of France was built over a series of reigns. Its famous 14th-century keep was for many years a state prison and retains the majesty of feudal architecture. Its inmates included the 18th-century philosopher Diderot.

The Sainte-Chapelle, which was completed in the 16th century, the royal pavilions, built by Le Vau for the young Louis XIV and for Anne of Austria, add the graciousness of a princely residence to the severity of a fortress.

Saint-Germain-en-Laye, on the other edge of the crown, was the cradle of Louis XIV, who

was born there in 1638. Five years later, Louis XIII died there. Louis XIV abandoned the Château-Neuf to Queen Elizabeth of England, the daughter of Marie de Médicis, and settled in the Château-Vieux which he altered by having Mansart enlarge it and build the long terrace which looks down over the Seine Valley. This was the scene of some memorable entertaining on a royal scale; eventually, however, Louis XIV left it and moved to Versailles.

The memory of Napoléon is much in evidence at La Malmaison, together with that of Joséphine de Beauharnais, who bought it in 1779, while she was the wife of General Bonaparte. Joséphine embellished this stately mansion, in which she was to experience both joy and sadness.

Ten years later, repudiated by the emperor, she withdrew to La Malmaison with her children and friends, and died there in 1814, as the empire was on the point of collapse. The following year Napoléon returned to the house before leaving for exile.

Marly-le-Roi was less fortunate. Louis XIV had Mansart build it as a hermitage where he could relax after the pomp and ceremony of Versailles. Louis XV neglected it. In a semi-ransacked condition, it was sold off at the Revolution to an industrialist who then went bankrupt, cut down the trees, sold off the marbles and even started removing the stonework of the château itself!

South of the capital, Chantilly and

Compiègne are of more recent origin. The Petit-Château de Chantilly was built by Jean Bullant for the Connétable Anne de Montmorency, and enlarged from 1876 to 1882 by the addition of the Grand-Château.

The Château de Compiègne in its present form dates from the late 18th century. It was the favorite residence of Napoléon III.

The noble castles of the Ile-de-France that surround the capital, forming what has been referred to as the "royal crown". Left: Vincennes, St.-Germain-en-Laye, la Malmaison. On the same page: Marly, Chantilly, and Compiègne.

ANCIENNE MAISON

CETTE MAISON, DITE ALORS
"AUX BILLARDS EN BOIS" EST CÉLÈBRE
DEPUIS 1850... FUT JUSQU'EN 1900,
LE LIEU DE RÉUNION DE DIAZ, PISSARO,
DEGAS, SYSLEY, CÉZANNE, T. LAUTREC,
RENOIR, MONET, E. ZOLA... SON JARDIN
SERVIT DE MODÈLE À VAN GOGH POUR SON
CHEF-D'OEUVRE "LA GUINGUETTE" QU'IL FIT
ICI EN OCTOBRE 1886, EXPOSÉ AU LOUVRE

X BILLARDS EN BOIS

DANS CETTE MAISON
Vincent VAN GOGH
A VÉCU
CHEZ SON FRÈRE THÉO
DE 1886 à 1888

MONTMARTRE...

Of the numerous windmills whose arms used to turn in the Montmartre sky, all that remains is two silhouettes, recently restored, as a symbol of the past.

Montmartre's past is so rich that whole volumes could be written about it. On this "martyrs' mount" Denys, Rustique and Eleuthere were beheaded for their faith; the local millers bravely resisted the Cossack onslaught of 1814; the last of the Communards sang of Montmartre in cherry blossom time...

Between the defense of country and liberty many years have elapsed. Besides being an essential part of the history of Paris, Montmartre is also a focal point of pleasure for Parisians and tourists alike. At the Moulin de la Galette Auguste Renoir painted the couples swirling beneath the fairy lights. Toulouse-Lautrec, at the Moulin Rouge, discovered La Goulue and Valentin le Désossé. Suzanne Valadon went from one mad love to the next and Maurice Utrillo, with a distant gaze, set up his easel in front of the white stone of Sacré Coeur, which was gradually rising above the Butte.

Montmartre has been prominent as a setting for the newly invigorated faith and for the goings-on of eternal youth, for the teeming intellectual life which flowed between the house of Mimi-Pinson and the Guinguette des Rapins, between the Chat Noir and the Lapin Agile, between Rodolphe Salis and Frede, the tavernkeeper of the Quai des Brumes, alternately comic and tragic. Montmartre was also the cradle of Cubism, where Picasso, on the Bateau-Lavoir, was preparing his own revolution...

Montmartre and the mill of La Galette. Renoir's house on the Allée des Brouillards (centerpage).

...AND MONTPARNASSE

Montparnasse all started at the Closerie des Lilas. At the beginning of the century, this establishment, still situated on the boundary between the Observatoire and the Boulevard, was merely a country dance hall — and its air was scented not by lilacs but by the linden blossoms of the neighboring convent gardens. Two poets, Andre Salmon and Paul Fort, planned to make the area an international centre for the arts and literature. Amazingly, they succeeded in doing just that, riding the uncontrollable wave of fashion which has played such an important part in shaping the city.

Just before the 1914 war, artists and bohemians began to desert Montmartre for the Left Bank, moving into the area between the Dome and the Rotonde, two cafes well placed in the artistic hierarchy. The academies, where a few masters of official art were still holding forth, saw the writing on the wall. Modigliani, the aristocrat from Livorno, had moved before the real exodus from Montmartre began. But it was the Russian plains and the Scandinavian or German forests that yielded the leaders of what was to become the Paris School, who settled in Montparnasse before 1914 : Chagall, Soutine, Zadkine, Kremegne, Kisling, as well as the Japanese Fujita, the Romanian Brancusi, the Mexican Rivera and many others.

A strange building — which has never ceased to serve the same purpose — houses most of these gifted emigrés : it was La Ruche (bechive), which had been built with the remnants of the 1900 Exposition. They, together with some

of their Parisian colleagues, turned Montparnasse into another lighthouse, whose brilliance was to radiate to the corners of the hemisphere.

Montparnasse: La Ruche, a point where painters of the Ecole de Paris congregated; the cafés that have become so well known for their artist clientele; Gauguin's studio (to the left on this floor of the building), rue de la Grande-Chaumière.

THE LUMIÈRE BROTHERS IN LYON, BIRTHPLACE OF THE MOVIE

The name Lumière (Fr. light) seems to have been predestined for involvement in the history of the cinema. Without light, the cinema could not exist. And the Lumière brothers, to-wards the end of the last century, were responsible for its sudden and spectacular growth!

The father of the two brothers was always eager to try new ideas. Having started as a sign painter, he later became a photographer and then a manufacturer of photo-sensitive plates. His sons developed his business and soon took an interest in research being done by French and American scientists in order to produce moving photographic images. A physiological phenomenon known since ancient times—mentioned by Lucretius, in fact—lay behind the origin of the motion picture: stroboscopy. The persistence of luminous impressions on the retina was to make it possible, by the use of a sequence of intermittent images, to obtain the illusion of continuous motion.

Jules Marey had developed the scientific analysis of movement by means of ultra-rapid snapshots. Edison, the inventor of the phonograph, devised the perforated film strip to keep it fixed. All that was needed was a way to move the strip intermittently so as to project the picture on a screen. Louis Lumière invented the system, during a sleepless night, and built the device known as the Cinematograph, which he patented on February 13, 1895. The cinema thus moved from the laboratory to actual practice. By synthesizing the results of their predecessors, the Lumière brothers laid the corner stone of the whole edifice. It is in that sense that they are sometimes referred to as the inventors of the cinema—a title which they never claimed for themselves. They came at the point of convergence of various lines of research which had been going on for more than a century. None of the equipment devised before them could assure the success of the invention. After them, all the problems were resolved. And Lyon now has a Rue du Premier Film!

Lyon and this patrician building in the Belle Epoque tradition were the intitial hosts of the Frères Lumière (Brothers Lumière) film promoters, whose studio has now been made into a museum (above and opposite).

THE EIFFEL TOWER, SYMBOL OF PARIS

In the eyes of the whole world it is the symbol of Paris. Ever since it was erected nearly

100 years ago as a result of the daring of a man of genius, its image has spread over the five continents: miniatures of iron, wood, mother-of-pearl, cardboard, nougat, chocolate, glass and other materials.

In 1886 the 54-year-old engineer Gustave Eiffel submitted his plans for a metal tower nearly 1,000 feet tall, to be the centerpiece of the 1889 Exposition. In return for a grant of 1 1/2 million francs Eiffel assumed full responsibility for the venture—including its financial aspects—and held exclusive rights to the operation of the tower for twenty years, after which it would revert to the City of Paris.

Work began on January 28, 1887. Two years and two months later, the gigantic structure was completed—nearly 7,000 tons of metal, 2 1/2 million bolts and rivets, 15,000 drawings for the assembly of the parts, and foundations covering 2 1/2 acres. The total cost: 7 1/2 million francs.

On March 31, 1889, Gustave Eiffel himself hoisted the French flag to the pinnacle of his skyscraper—the first ever, and at the time the tallest structure in the world.

To begin with, the Eiffel Tower was severely criticized, scorned and insulted, particularly by artists and high society; indeed several decades had to elapse before this mass of iron was recognized as having the two things which many people had stubbornly denied it: elegance and beauty.

The Eiffel Tower and the monumental vista afforded from the Trocadéro Fountains, with the Champ de Mars and the Military Academy. Beneath the endless mass of steel ribbing, the bust of the designer-engineer (right).

THE SOURCES OF INSPIRATION

Throughout France there are a certain number of privileged places which have been immortalized on canvas by the new vision of the impressionists and post-impressionists, in the 19th century. This great moment in French painting revealed to the world the interplay of light on things, and the palpitation of appearances beneath the instability of the atmosphere.

Claude Monet, on the borders of Ile-de-France and Normandy, chose mills and poplar trees as the subjects of his paintings, in which the theme is actually nothing more than a pretext for an endless series of nuances according to the hour and the season. His searching mind reacted in the same way outside Rouen Cathedral and in the steam of the Gare Saint-Lazare. But it was at Giverny, with his *Water Lilies,* that Claude Monet took his magical command of colors to its highest point.

He settled in the Epte Valley in 1883,

renovated his house and turned the barn into a studio, dug a pond and designed a garden which was, in turn, destined to play a creative part in the formation of his astonishing chromatic poems.

The house and the garden have recently been restored and opened to the public. Visitors can see mementos from the painter's life and the floral beauty which was his source of inspiration until his death.

Light was also the driving force behind Vincent Van Gogh, who went from his native Brabant to Paris, and thence to Arles, where he discovered what he called his "Japan"... so greatly was he impressed by the brightness of the sun shining on the almond blossom and its exotic overtones. Here his art reached its zenith, in a surge of exaltation which revealed to him the cosmic vision of the universe, thus causing him, briefly, to lose control of his own reason.

In the "little yellow house" in Arles, in the cell at Saint-Rémy-de-Provence—since destroyed by war and neglect—Vincent Van Gogh the

visionary raised pictorial art beyond its previous limits.

What Van Gogh sought in space, his friend Paul Gauguin could be said to have sought in time. At the foot of the Breton calvaries, on the ancient soil of Armor, at Pont-Aven and Le Pouldu, he was already probing for the true origins of being and of life, as he was to do later at Tahiti.

Another man with a passionate quest was Paul Cézanne, in Provence, gazing at the "rocks of fire" of the Montagne Sainte-Victoire.

Left: reminder of Gauguin at Pont-Aven with, below, the famous Pont de l'Anglois in Arles that was immortalized by Van Gogh. Below: Monet's garden and the courtyard of his house in Giverny, Normandy. Below as well: Mont Sainte-Victoire, of which Cézanne was so fond, and Cézanne's own house in Aix-en-Provence.

VERDUN, THE TOWN OF SACRIFICE

What a hell it was! The most atrocious battle of all time: ten months of fierce fighting, 400,000 French soldiers killed in this gigantic holocaust — 300,000 of them without a grave — and vast numbers of Germans.

With its strategic location, Verdun had always been an important fortress, holding the key to the Eastern Marches. If it had fallen in 1916, the French hinterland would doubtless have been defenseless, as in 1940. As early as the first year of the war the French defenses at Verdun had withstood the enemy onslaught. In February 1916 a sudden attack on a massive scale enabled Germans to encircle the Bois de Caures, where Lieutenant-Colonel Driant fell with his force of light infantry, and seize Douaumont Fort. The action spread to the left bank of the Meuse towards the Mort-Homme. For weeks the French resistance fought stubbornly to hold Fort Vaux and the Cote 304. General Petain, the commander of the army at Verdun, was replaced in May by General Nivelle, and the battle continued its erratic course.

Early in September the enemy was driven back all along the front, and on October 24 a French assault recovered in four hours the ground which the Germans had spent months acquiring. Forts Douaumont and Vaux were nothing but ruins by this time, but they were nonetheless recaptured; the offensives conducted by General Mangin returned the front line to its initial position by December.

The German offensive had thus served no purpose. The French victory, though costly, had saved the country from a general invasion. Being a defensive victory against an attacking force, it was all the more meritorious. Victories based on conquest are often suspect and are always deplorable, as they inevitably lead to more fighting. At Verdun, the French soldiers were defending their own home territory, and their freedom.

By the time the fighting was over, the town of Verdun was a pile of rubble. All that had survived was a part of the ramparts, as well as some monuments which have since been patiently restored. Reconstruction was long and difficult,

but Verdun has come to life again, with its upper town.

For French veterans and the young generation it has become a moving pilgrimage. It is possible to take a guided tour of Forts Vaux and Douaumont, the trenches, the Mort-Homme and the national military cemetery, where so many anonymous heroes lie buried.

Verdun: the « Tranchée des baïonnettes » (Trench of the Bayonets), the Douaumont ossuary, and two old field cannon... the memorable and tragic setting of the most terrible battle of all time.

SAINT-TROPEZ – PAINTERS,
POETS AND STARS

Known affectionately as Saint-Trop' to regulars, this small port in the south of France, where the fishing boats bob at anchor on a perenially blue sea, has become *the* place to be seen during the summer months.

Before it became a high-class marina for stars of many firmaments and vacationing millionares, Saint-Tropez was favored by painters. Paul Signac – who with Seurat was the apostle of pictorial divisionism – was passionately fond of the sea and of boats. He owned a succession of 32 yachts and decided one day to set off on a voyage around the world. His first port of call was Saint-Tropez... and he went no further!

He fell in love with the tiny harbor and the peninsula, bought a house and proceeded to invite all his friends to join him. For a while Saint-Tropez became the capital of pointillism. The charming Musée de l'Annonciade, near the harbor, contains works of Signac, Admond Cross and other painters enamoured of lighting effects: Matisse, Marquet, Vuillard, Bonnard, Dufy. Certain views of the harbors at Marseille, Cassis and Saint-Tropez, signed by Paul Signac, are orchestrated displays of color which embrace the entire rainbow!

Dunoyer de Segonzac was also a regular at Saint-Tropez, where he produced his brilliant etchings for Colette's novel *La Treille Muscate,* which was also the name of the author's house.

Before becoming the social resort town we know it to be today, Saint Tropez was actually an artists' retreat: Signac drew on the colors of the bay, for example; and the former Castle of Antibes (right) has been made into the Picasso Museum.

THE PICASSO MUSEUM AT ANTIBES

Antibes — the Antipolis of the ancient Greeks, founded in the 5th century BC — was an important commercial port serving Massilia (Marseille) and Italy. Much ancient pottery has been recovered from the sea bed in this area. Two thousand years later, situated at the frontier between France and the State of Savoy, Antibes was fortified by Vauban, who built its ramparts and the Square Fort, solidly facing out to sea.

In 1946, the château Grimaldi, with its Romanesque tower, was offered to the inventive genius of Picasso, who was living in Vallauris at the time. He set up his studio on the third floor and started work with his varied materials. Here he was to produce some major works, in which Antipolis had a symbolic value: flowers became women, goats and satyrs, while geometric shapes came to life.

The Picasso Museum, which is superbly laid out on three well-lit floors, provides the most eloquent overall view of the artist's mature work. After the period of destruction which followed the *Demoiselles d'Avignon,* here we have a flowering of shapes and colors on the mythological themes which then haunted him. The flute-playing satyrs, the thread-like nymphs, the goats and bulls, fishes and sea-urchins dance an astonishing ballet. Rather than actual things, Picasso depicts the idea behind those things, as perceived by his creative fantasy. His extraordinary diversity and prodigious powers of invention are displayed in an abundance of oils and gouaches, charcoal sketches, pencil drawings, ceramics pottery and sculpture. This art is not a quest, nor an expression but a delightful form of play—very much as the ancient Greeks of Antipolis would have understood the word.

THE BORDELAIS WINE MUSEUMS

Between the Gironde and the Atlantic, the Médoc region stretches for over 1,700 acres, with its highly reputed vineyards: Saint-Estèphe, Margaux and a number of famous "châteaux".

The quays of the small industrial town of Pauillac, extend along the estuary. This is the point of departure, for the whole world, of the French ambassador with a heady aroma—the wine of Bordeaux. There is a museum in its honor, run by the Commanderie de Bontemps-Médoc, whose privileged members engage in festivities which are in no way less splendid than those of the Tastevin de Bourgogne!

Among these select *crus,* Mouton-Lafitte, north of Pauillac, was renowned as early as the 14th century. In those days the barony of Mouton belonged to the Sire de Pons, who ceded it in the 15th to the dukes of Gloucester and of Dunois and then to Gaston de Foix, while in the 16th century the estate passed to the dukes of Joyeuse and Epernon—all of them nobles of the highest lineage.

In 1740 the property was divided: Mouton became separate from Lafitte and was henceforth part of the fief of Baron de Brane, until it was bought in 1853 by Baron Nathaniel de Rothschild.

Two years later a hierarchy was established by the vintners of the region in order to determine the value of the *grands crus.* Château de Mouton-Rothschild was classified second, much to the dismay of its owner, who declared, thus formulating his own motto: "Premier ne suis, second ne veux, Mouton je suis" (I am not first, I will not be second, I am a Mouton).

The hierarchy changed nothing about the order of merit, and Mouton-Rothschild continued to make the top grades in tests of Bordeaux wines throughout the world.

In 1793 the list was revised, with the result

that Mouton-Rothschild ranked first. And Baron Philippe de Rothschild, partly echoing his ancestor, proudly changed the motto to read: "Premier je suis, second je fus. Mouton ne change".

The 173 acres of the ancient barony were being given credit for their true quality. The victory was recorded by the establishment of a museum which would proclaim, for visitors from all over the world, the rich past of the *appellation* and its present brilliance. It was laid out by the baron himself, in disused wine cellars. On flagstones from the early period of the vineyard, glass display cases show splendid *objets d'art* inspired or created by wine since ancient times: Sassanid

gold goblets, Egyptian alabaster cups, Persian ceramics, Venetian glass of the 18th century and a collection of thousands of bottles of every sort.

A sampling of Bordeaux « Grand Cru ». Above: the Château St.-Georges vineyards in Saint-Emilion. Left: Mouton-Lafite, and, above: the Château Beychevelle grounds, with, opposite: the Château de Margaux vineyards.

CLOS-VOUGEOT, THE REALM OF WINE

"Oh disinherited Man, I bring you
In my prison of glass and my scarlet wax,
A song full of light and friendship!"

In these words the poet Baudelaire sang his own hymn of gratitude to the "soul of wine". If

France is, above all others, *the* country of wine — or rather of *wines* — the Chateau de Clos-Vougeot is its most venerable temple!

This magnificent Renaissance mansion was restored in the 19th century, but the Chapter Rooms and the Great Cellar date from the 12th and 13th centuries. They were owned at that time

by the Cistercian monks. Clos-Vougeot, situated in the heart of the Burgundy wine country, and standing proudly amongst the vineyards which surround it, conjures up a picture of nearly a thousand years of triumphant wine-making.

In 1110 Abbé Alberic, of the Cistercian Order, organized the community, appointing lay

brothers to perform certain material tasks. These included the reclamation of fallow land: forty years later the vineyards were already flourishing.

After an eclipse in the 15th century the Cistercians renovated the estate and the 48th abbot, Dom Loisier, built the residence, of which it has been said that "the massive exterior brings to mind the notion of a fortress, while the interior suggests the still somewhat disorderly refinements of the Renaissance".

The 1789 Revolution dealt the death blow to the estate. It was put up for auction and awarded to an incompetent. Some decades later, however, Clos-Vougeot had recovered its full renown — to such an extent that the Duc d'Aumale, on his return from Italy, felt obliged to respect the tradition whereby

"When you go to Vougeot, respectfully,
You must present arms to the fertile vine
Which will give birth to the king of all wines".

Since 1944 the chateau and the estate have been the property of the Confrérie des Chevaliers du Tastevin, founded ten years earlier by the vintners of the Côtes de Beaune region. The introduction of new members takes place annually at a ceremony in the Great cellar, attended by numerous guests. After knocking three times to be admitted into the "first circle of wine", the initiate must follow a precise ritual. Surrounded by the Knights in their traditional robes and caps, the newcomer swears allegiance to the Bacchic

The celebrated ritual of the Confrérie du Tastevin (Winetasting Brotherhood) in Burgundy (right), a ceremony which takes place in this elegant hall of the Clos-Vougeot Castle. In the outer court, a monument to the winemaker.

order which, under the triple patronage of Noe, Bacchus and Saint Vincent, has more than three thousand members — ambassadors, academicians, artists and gastronomes — scattered about the world.

A sumptuous banquet is followed by Bacchic singing, under the banners which bear the motto of the Confraternity:

"Jamais en vain... Toujours en vin" (Never in vain, always in wine).

The castle estates that have yielded the « Grand Cru » of Burgundy: Clos-Vougeot, Meursault, and, opposite, Aloxe-Corton.

THE BATTLE OF VERCORS

Between the Isère and the Drôme there is a high plateau of pastures, ringed by forests and sealed off by two mountains ranges over 6,500 feet high. This natural fortress was chosen in 1943 by the French Resistance to Nazi occupation as a center for training and for clandestine operations.

In the spring of 1944 more than 4,000 underground resistance fighters were assembled in this sector, access to which was so difficult as to apparently preclude enemy inflitration. In two months a large-scale offensive managed, however, to crush the heroic resistance of the valiant force at Vercors.

On June 13 the Germans attacked and burned Saint-Nizier. Bombardments became more intense. Airbone troops were dropped into the center of the massif, with heavy fighting at Vassieux, La Mure and Les Chaux. At the Valchevrière Belvedere Lieutenant Chabal and his light infantry were overwhelmed, while the Senegalese sharpshooters did not fare much better at Saint-Martin-en-Vercors.

On July 23, faced with a hopeless situation, Colonel Huet gave the order to disperse. Seriously wounded patients from the hospital at Saint-Martin were moved into the Luire Caves by doctors and nurses. Four days later they were discovered there by the Germans and massacred.

The Battle of Vercors was lost as far as the underground resistance was concerned, but their bravery, by pinning down the enemy, had helped the landing of the Allies in Provence. Several months later, Vercors was free.

The Vercors mountain range has become another of the nation's historic sites as a result of the activities of the French Resistance here during the last world war. Left: the Memorial in Vassieux-en-Vercors.

THE D-DAY BEACHES

In the coded language of the Allies they were known as Utah, Omaha, Gold, Juno, Sword, stretched out along the Calvados coast better known in those days for its quiet family beaches and tiny fishing harbors: Port-en-Bessin, Arromanches, Saint-Aubin-sur-Mer, Muc-sur-Mer, etc.

On June 6, 1944, at dawn, the most colossal military operation of all time got under way. Hundreds of naval craft − cruisers, tugs, dredgers − opened the way for more than 4,000 ships and landing craft from which the British and Canadian divisions and the Free French Forces were to set foot on the Continent, while American airbone troops were dropped over the two wings of the sector, particularly at Sainte-Mère-Eglise. And it was there, on June 6, 1964, twenty years after the landings, that a museum, symbolically shaped like a parachute, was inaugurated. The landings on the beaches were commemorated at Arromanches.

Between Colleville-sur-Mer and Vierville-sur-Mer, the 10,000 marble tombstones of the Saint-Laurent cemetery convey something of the magnitude of the sacrifices made in the name of freedom from tyranny.

On this page: the coast and former scene of the Allies' Normandy Invasion with, as persistent reminders: Utah Beach, Omaha Beach and its American cemetery, and the little church of Sainte-Mère-Eglise on which steeple a paratrooper is known to have landed.

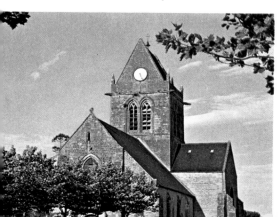

SAINT-GERMAIN-DES-PRÉS: THE SPIRIT OF AN AGE

Ever since the beginning of the century, Saint-Germain-des-Prés, between the old academic district and the antique shops and galleries, has symbolized the intellectual life of Paris. It is a village church in the heart of the capital, a crossroads of the Left Bank which is also a meeting-place for ideas; little remains, however, of the *prés* (meadows) of its name.

As early as 1900 the Café de Flore was a favorite with the nostalgic royalists of the Action Française, led by Charles Maurras. Later on, the Brasserie Lipp, on the other bank of the boule-vard, was frequented by writers and politicians: Edouard Herriot and Léon Blum, Paul Valéry and Jean Giraudoux, Saint-Exupéry and Max Jacob. And in 1933 the Café des Deux-Magots founded a literary prize in its name.

But it was particularly after the liberation of Paris that Saint-Germain-des-Prés really became a new center of the intellectual world. It was the birthplace and home of a philosophical theory —existentialism—which was to overflow its confines in order to become, for a society which had for too long been bullied by the constraints of war and occupation, a highly fashionable way of thinking, an emancipation of behavior.

Jean-Paul Sartre was the pontiff of the

movement. With Simone de Beauvoir, Albert Camus, Merleau-Ponty, Jean Genet and others, he was to be involved in the changing patterns of thought which involved the various sociological and political trends of the post-war period.

In a film which became something of a landmark, *Rendez-vous de Juillet,* Jacques Becker showed the youth of the post-war period torn between *joie de vivre* and the difficulty of actually being. In his words: "The important thing is to have found a whole generation struggling with the material impediments of life—people for whom bourgeois prosperity was a dead letter, who had broken their bonds and were determined to experience an adventure of their own making."

This adventure was to be sought by these young people in the "caves" (cellars), whose fame was soon to spread well beyond Paris. On April 11, 1947, the Tabou opened its doors on Rue Dauphine, where the cream of Paris society was invited. Before becoming the spokesman of the next generation, Boris Vian played the trumpet there, while Juliette Gréco sang poems by Raymond Queneau and Jacques Prévert. The Tabou was rivalled by the Rose Rouge—a genuine temple of existentialism. The rhythms, which were largely of American origin, followed each other into oblivion in swift succession—be-bop, swing, and then rock.

Saint-Germain-des-Prés has lost most of its "caves", but it still has its cafés—Le Flore, Les Deux-Magots, Chez Lipp—as well as its artists and its poets.

Saint-Germain-des-Prés: in post-war years people claimed that there were more geniuses here per square foot than in any other spot in the world. One tends to forget that the interior of the church is also quite beautiful.

COLOMBEY-LES-DEUX-EGLISES

In 1938, having been promoted to the rank of colonel the year before, Charles de Gaulle, with an eye to his later years, bought the estate of La Boisserie, at Colombey-les-Deux-Eglises, a village in the Est region, in a clearing surrounded by forests. That same year he published *France and Her Army;* in 1939 he was entrusted with the command of the tank brigade of the fifth army.

From then on, aware of the inevitability of war, he disagreed with the Chiefs of Staff over problems of national defense. The war which did eventually take place confirmed his beliefs. On January 26, 1940, he addressed a memorandum, *The Coming of Mechanized Warfare,* which defined his strategy. The invasion proved him right. On June 5, 1940, summoned by President Reynaud to the Defense Ministry, de Gaulle moved from the military sphere into politics; but he refused to consider an armistice. "I can conceive of an army capitulating, but the State does not capitulate." Then followed the appeal of June 18, delivered from London, for the resumption of the fight.

After the Allied victory, General de Gaulle withdrew to La Boisserie from 1946 to 1958, when his country once more called for him. Then, for another ten years he was fighting again, but this time in the political sphere.

Ten years—indeed as long as there was confidence in him. "I shall leave public affairs before they leave me. The sea recedes, but de Gaulle will not allow himself to be buried in quicksand." It should be noted that he was here talking about himself in the third person, as if actually witnessing his own glory.

Among the many works written about General de Gaulle, his life, his career, his mission and his ideas, the one by Frederic Barreyre, *The General's Last Words,* is an astonishing portrait—a kind of filigree—of this ambitious, determined and courageous man who, for more than a quarter of a century, truly identified himself with his country.

Through the repartee and the quips related by the author, one can catch a glimpse of the pride of a man who knew that he was designated by destiny for great things, his contempt for everyone else, including those who worked by his side, his sense of grandeur and the consequent scorn he felt for everything "secondary". In May 1968, during the severe student unrest, he spoke of a "revolt of high-school seniors"—an expression which suggests an inability to grasp the greatness of movements which emanate from the people.

"Now listen to this, Mr. Curate, the English are wrong to compare me to Napoléon; he spoilt his exit, and I will tell you why: it is because he was unable to choose correctly either the place or the hour of his defeat. Not so in my case."

He retired once again to La Boisserie, this time for good. "This is my home. In the tumult of men and events, solitude was my temptation. Now it is my friend. What other friend will suffice when one has encountered History?"

He went walking in the woods, wrote his war memoirs, consulted the cards. On November 9, 1970, he collapsed at his table.

The impressive Croix de Lorraine (Lorraine Cross) mounted atop one of the ridges at Colombey-les-deux-Eglises in memory of General de Gaulle. The following inscription is to be read at the base of the monument: "A fullscore centuries' pact has bound up the greatness of France with the freedom of the world." Seen below, the General's estate, La Boisserie, and the surrounding woods where he was wont to reflect.

"BEAUBOURG", OR THE CENTRE GEORGES POMPIDOU

"I so much want Paris to have its own cultural center— one combining a museum and a center for creativity, in which the plastic arts would be housed under the same roof as music, the cinema, books and audio-visual research."

These words of President Pompidou, from a ministerial meeting of 1969, led to the decision, in December of that year, to build such a center on the Plateau Beaubourg, in the heart of Old Paris.

The 1970 international competition, which attracted a total of 681 designs, was won by a group of three architects—two Italians and an Englishman. Clearing of the site started in 1972, and five years later the project was completed. The Centre, which was opened to the public on February 2, 1977, covers an area of 25 acres and cost 993 million francs to build.

At the same time the old district of Saint-Merri was renovated. The tall façades of 17th— and 18th—century houses, once the maze of narrow streets had been cleared away, suddenly appeared in their full beauty, accross the gently sloping forecourt leading to the Centre. In two years, from February 1977 to February 1979, the total number of free admissions came to 12,756,702.

Every day of the week, in fair weather or foul, a constant flow of visitors—of all races and from all levels of society—feeds into the escalators at the foot of the building and is deposited at the top of this strange mass of tubular steel which has earned the Centre the nickname of "The Refinery".

The forecourt itself has become a sort of *agora,* where the performing arts are always present in one form or another: Latin American musicians, black dancers, fire-eaters, jugglers, portrait artists and mimes, some of whom are excellent. The spectators mill around in a general

carnival-like atmosphere. In this way, outside the most modern building in Paris, the medieval street, with its buskers and tumblers, has come to life again.

There is no doubt about it: the Centre Pompidou attracts more visitors than any other public building in Paris. It is a sort of Luna-Park of culture, with exhibits, a richly endowed library on three floors, movie theatres and a bookshop.

It has also attracted a unique amount of criticism, not only of its structural design, but of the effects of its "mission". In a short and sharply worded publication, Jean Baudrillard has written the indictment of the Centre and its underlying conception: "Using a museum-like scenario which merely preserves the humanistic fiction of culture, what is really happening at Beaubourg is the death of culture: the masses are joyously invited to attend a *cultural mourning session.* And they come in their droves.

Assorted glimpses of the Centre Pompidou at Beaubourg and the plaza in front of the building. On the following pages: one village in France, similar to so many thousands of others, set in the midst of the vineyards.